Profitable Patterns for Stock Trading

by

Larry Pesavento

TRADERS PRESS®
INCORPORATED
PO BOX 6206
GREENVILLE, SC 29606

Books and Gifts for
Traders and Investors.

Copyright© 1999 by Larry Pesavento
ISBN# 0-934380-47-3
Published January 1999

TRADERS PRESS®
INCORPORATED
PO BOX 6206
GREENVILLE, SC 29606

Books and Gifts for
Traders and Investors.

Dedication

~~To Benida~~
The one who knows all about me
~the good, the bad, and the ugly
and she still loves me—
unconditionally!

TRADERS PRESS, INC.®
PO BOX 6206
Greenville, SC 29606
Books and Gifts
for Investors and Traders

Publishers of:

A Complete Guide to Trading Profits (Paris)
A Professional Look at S&P Day Trading (Trivette)
Beginner's Guide to Computer Assisted Trading (Alexander)
Channels and Cycles: A Tribute to J.M. Hurst (Millard)
Chart Reading for Professional Traders (Jenkins)
Commodity Spreads: Analysis, Selection and Trading Techniques (Smith)
Comparison of Twelve Technical Trading Systems (Lukac, Brorsen, & Irwin)
Day Trading with Short Term Price Patterns (Crabel)
Fibonacci Ratios with Pattern Recognition (Pesavento)
Geometry of Stock Market Profits (Jenkins)
Harmonic Vibrations (Pesavento)
How to Trade in Stocks (Livermore)
Hurst Cycles Course (J.M. Hurst)
Jesse Livermore: Speculator King (Sarnoff)
Magic of Moving Averages (Lowry)
Planetary Harmonics of Speculative Markets (Pesavento)
Point & Figure Charting (Aby)
Point & Figure Charting: Commodity and Stock Trading Techniques (Zieg)
Profitable Grain Trading (Ainsworth)
Reminiscences of a Stock Operator (Lefevre)
Stock Market Trading Systems (Appel & Hitschler)
Stock Patterns for Stock Trading (Rudd)
Study Helps in Point & Figure Techniques (Wheelan)
Technically Speaking (Wilkinson)
Technical Trading Systems for Commodities and Stocks (Patel)
The Professional Commodity Trader (Kroll)
The Taylor Trading Technique (Taylor)
The Traders (Kleinfeld)
*The Trading Rule That Can Make You Rich** (Dobson)
Traders Guide to Technical Analysis (Hardy)
Trading Secrets of the Inner Circle (Goodwin)
Trading S&P Futures and Options (Lloyd)
Understanding Bollinger Bands (Dobson)
Understanding Fibonacci Numbers (Dobson)
Viewpoints of a Commodity Trader (Longstreet)
Wall Street Ventures & Adventures Through Forty Years (Wyckoff)
Winning Market Systems (Appel)

Please contact **Traders Press** to receive our current 100 page catalog describing these and many other books and gifts of interest to investors and traders.

800-927-8222 ~ Fax 864-298-0221 ~ 864-298-0222 ~ tradersprs@aol.com
http://www.traderspress.com

Visit our Website at http://www.traderspress.com

• View our latest releases
• Browse our updated catalog
• Access our Gift Shop for investors
• Read our book reviews

Contact us for our hardcopy 100 page catalog.

TRADERS PRESS, INC.™
PO Box 6206
Greenville, SC 29606

Tradersprs@aol.com

800-927-8222

Fax 864-298-0222

Preface

Over the past 20 years the use and misuse of the Fibonacci Summation series has proliferated to the point that commentators on the nation's TV business channels are now resident experts. I lay no claim to being an expert. I have, however, studied the subject of Fibonacci numbers extensively, especially how it relates to trading. I have always taken the pragmatic position that if I could not use what I was studying to help in trading, then I was not interested in pursuing it any further. If this material can stimulate your interest in the subject, then introducing you to the subject will have been worthwhile. A word of caution, this material is based on the probabilities of trading. The art of trading is one of risk management. Amos Hostetter, one of the founders of Commodity Corporation in Princeton, New Jersey, used to say, *"Take care of losses and the profits will take care of themselves."* I use this quote a lot because I believe it is very important!

The pattern recognition methodology illustrated in the text will be of interest to anyone that has ever traded using technical charts. I can say with confidence that there are very few who have researched patterns to the extent I have. Some of the references date back to the early 1900s. Each of these patterns is based on ratio and proportion. A technical chart is nothing more than a road map with a price and time axis. These patterns repeat with a great deal of regularity. Some of my best students have been airline pilots. They seem to approach trading like they approach flying, following a flight plan. The similarities to trading are numerous.

Finally, one of my goals in writing this book is to expose you to the subject of ancient geometry. Fibonacci numbers are an integral part of the numbers that make up the subject of ancient geometry. It will be of interest to some of you that many of these sacred ratios have their origin in the cosmos. I will not spend a significant amount of time relating my experiences in astro-harmonics research. The subject is too vast for me to consider here. More importantly, it is not necessary for profitable trading.

Acknowledgments

Special thanks to Edward Dobson, President of **Traders Press** for publishing this book.

Special thanks to Sharon Lewis for her numerous hours of compiling data to make this book possible.

I am very grateful to Margaret Ros Hudson and Teresa Darty Alligood from **Traders Press** for readying this book for its debut. I would also like to recognize the artistic efforts of these two ladies in the creation of this bookcover.

Contents

Introduction xi

Harmonic and Vibratory Numbers 1

Geometrics of a Price Chart 13

The Primary Patterns 21

Classical Chart Patterns Using Ratio and Proportion 71

Bonus Pattern: The Butterfly 83

The Opening Price 89

Entry Techniques 97

It's Different This Time 103

The Non Random Nature of Chaos Theory 115

Appendices 133

   I   Description of the Gartley "222" Pattern ... 133

   II   Some Practical Tips on Cycles 150

   III   Some More Practical Tips on Cycles 155

   IV   Additional Reading 160

Introduction

Leonardo de Pisa de Fibonacci and Beyond

On the eastern seaboard of Italy, about an hour's drive from Florence, lies the town of Pisa. It was here that Fibonacci was born. He was a thirteenth century mathematician who primarily worked for the royal families of Italy. The work for which he is most famous is the *Libre Abaci* (Book of Calculations). His award for this work was the present day equivalent of the Nobel Peace Prize. Fibonacci was largely responsible for the use of arithmetic numbers versus Roman numerals. Before Fibonacci, the number 30 was written XXX. After his *Libre Abaci*, it was written 30.

Legend describes his journey to Egypt as one of great discoveries. He went to Egypt to study the mathematical relationships contained in the pyramids.

Those of you who really want to study the math contained in the pyramids should read Peter Thompkin's book *The Secret of the Great Pyramids*. It is not my intention to explore all of the geometry in the pyramids, only the Fibonacci Summation series. Fibonacci found this series when he studied the Great Pyramid at Giza. **The series is the sum of the two previous numbers 0, 1, 1, 2, 3, 5, 8, 13, 21, 34, 55, 89, 144 to infinity. Dividing one number by the next after the eighth sequence yields 21÷ 34 = .618.** This just happens to be the relationship of the height of the Great Pyramid to its base.

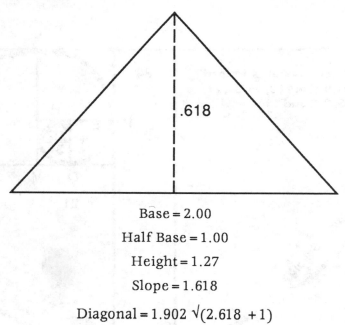

Base = 2.00

Half Base = 1.00

Height = 1.27

Slope = 1.618

Diagonal = 1.902 $\sqrt{(2.618 + 1)}$

This additive series of numbers is based on the equation: Phi + 1 = Phi squared ($\phi + 1 = \phi^2$).

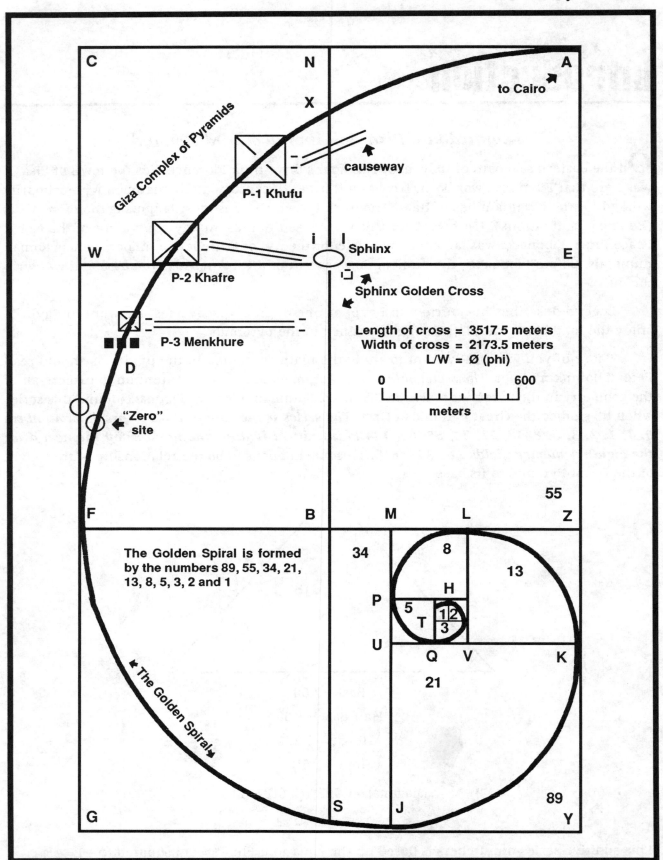

C N X A
to Cairo

Giza Complex of Pyramids

causeway

P-1 Khufu

W i I Sphinx E

P-2 Khafre

Sphinx Golden Cross

P-3 Menkhure

Length of cross = 3517.5 meters
Width of cross = 2173.5 meters
L/W = Ø (phi)

D

0   600

"Zero" site

meters

55

F B M L Z

The Golden Spiral is formed
by the numbers 89, 55, 34, 21,
13, 8, 5, 3, 2 and 1

34

8

13

P

H

5

1 2

T

3

The Golden Spiral

U

Q V K

21

G S J 89

Y

What Fibonacci did for me was to open my eyes! These are the relationships that are constantly in the market. I first started using Fibonacci numbers in 1974 at the urging of John Hill, Sr. of the Commodity Research Institute of Hendersonville North Carolina. I read all of Elliott's papers and his correspondence with Charles Collins. Years later, Frost and Prechter wrote the book *Elliott Wave Theory,* which explained the wave structure and the use of Fibonacci numbers. It concerned me that not all the waves were .382, .500, .618, 1.618. It was not until 1988 that I began using the square root numbers of the Fibonacci series $\sqrt{.618}$ = .786 and $\sqrt{1.618}$ = 1.27. Armed with these two square root relationships, the wave structure can be more easily explained. Bryce Gilmore's first book, *Geometry of Markets*, brought the ratios to the public's attention. *The Elliott Wave Newsletter* has never used these ratios as far as I know. I used to fax information to them on the square root numbers, but they never responded. Robert Miner of the Dynamic Traders Group in Tucson, Arizona, uses all of the harmonic ratios. It is my opinion that his newsletter and technical work is the best in our business. If you don't have the time to do the work, Robert Miner, one of the best technicians on this planet, will do it for you at a small monthly cost. This reminds me of one of my favorite quotes from my friend and fellow trader, Jim Twentyman *"Defy Human Nature—Do the work yourself."*

What this book is going to do is illustrate how to use the Fibonacci ratios, their square roots, and their reciprocals to determine the structure of wave vibrations. Of all the books I have in my library, none of the Elliott Wave material covers this important concept. I am going to keep it as simple as possible. If you can glean only one or two concepts or patterns, then this material will not have been written in vain. I can promise you this much. If you study the ratios and patterns shown here, you will realize that markets have a definite pattern hidden within their chaos. Sorting through this chaos can enlighten you. The goal here is not to try to predict the future or even to know what is going to happen next. No one knows that! (Well, there is One who knows, but He doesn't trade.) It is not necessary to know what is going to happen in 5 days. What is necessary is to determine how much risk and profit potential is available in the next 5 days. Probability is the name of the game. Risk control is of tantamount importance. Winners think in terms of how much they can lose. Losers focus on how much they can win. *"Take care of your losses and the profits will take care of themselves."* —A.B.H.

By the time I have finished, I hope you will see **the correlation of geometric patterns to the ratios and proportions illustrated**. It is going to be as simple as I can make it for you. Should you want more elaborate reading material it will be listed in the bibliography.

The material here has always proven exciting to me and my fellow traders who also subscribe to this approach to the market. In my opinion, it answers the question, *"Can there be order in the chaos of the market?"* I wish I could have known this much about the market 20 years ago!

One more thought about the square root number from the golden mean. These numbers were first revealed in William Garrett's incredible book *The Torque Analysis of Stock Market Cycles.* This is hands-down the best book on cycles I have ever read. There were only 200 copies sold in 1972. The remainder were destroyed by Prentice-Hall due to lack of interest. The book was recently republished by Ruff Publishing (509-448-6739). An excellent choice for every library.

There are a lot of charts in this book. I know of no other way to illustrate these concepts. Charts were selected from all areas, from commodities to the Dow Jones stocks. Several different time frames were selected because these patterns are found in all time frames.

Do not be disappointed if you do not see the traditional Elliott Wave pattern labeling. It is not neccesary when you are using short term pattern recognition. **What is important is the ratio and proportion of each wave.** Frankly, I never felt too comfortable about exactly identifying the precise Elliott Wave count. This was brought to my attention most vividly several years ago at my trading house in Pismo Beach, California. Bryce Gilmore and Robert Miner were discussing T-Bonds. They both came up with different Elliott Wave counts. They humbly admitted that they were *both right*! And these are two of the best technicians I have ever met. Bryce introduced the technician to the true geometry of the market, with his software program and book, *Wave Trader*. I count him as one of my very good friends and I will always be indebted to him. Although Elliott Wave devotees may cringe at this thought, you need not be overly concerned with wave labeling, but the square roots and their reciprocals can go a long way in analyzing a wave in the true Elliott sense.

Harmonic and Vibratory Numbers

I included the section on Harmonic and Vibratory numbers early in this book so the reader will begin to think in terms of repetitions and swings.

Reluctance to share some of their most precious trading secrets is probably inherent in all traders. I am no exception. What you will observe in this chapter is, in my opinion, one of the best kept secrets in technical analysis. These harmonic, or vibratory numbers as I refer to them, can be incredibly useful for profit projection and stop placement. Every commodity, stock, or speculative instrument has its own vibratory number. It is as natural as each element on a chemical chart having its own number. Traders who specialize in trading one speculative vehicle use these numbers all the time. They don't know why, except that they repeat day after day. The next few pages and charts will describe these numbers and illustrate their usage. Make no mistake about this section: it could be one of the most effective tools you can use as a trader.

My first interest in these harmonic or vibratory numbers occurred in 1979 while I was operating the commodity department for Drexel Burnham Lambert in southern California. Jim Twentyman was working with me and occupied the adjoining office. A small window was located between the offices so we could talk without using the phone. Jim had just moved from Conti Commodities where he was a very successful broker/trader. He was now helping me manage my C.T.A. firm, A.V.M. Associates. Jim purchased a Wang computer in 1977 to do research on cycles and numbers. He also took a two year sabbatical to study the works of the legendary trader W.D. Gann.

I had access to the library of the Invest-ment Center Bookstore in West Los Angeles. This library had the finest collection of books that I had ever seen. Any book that I ever heard about was there, including rare astrological books and old technical books from the 1920s and 1930s. Once you go through this vintage material you will realize there is not a lot that is new to technical analysis. Most assuredly there are new concepts and ideas, but most material can be traced back to earlier traders. I think you will agree that the concept of harmonic or vibratory numbers fits into the "new idea" bracket.

The easiest way to describe why harmonic numbers work the way they do is to use an analogy. Suppose you were to drop a rock into a pool of water. (See illustration below.) Once the rock hits the water, waves will vibrate from the center of impact until the

Why Harmonic Numbers Work

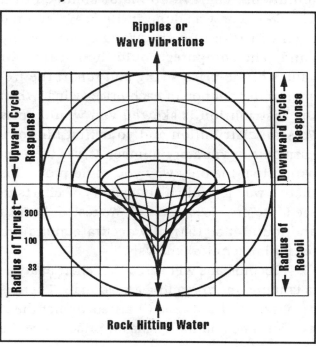

thrust of the rock hitting the water dissipates. There are four things that will determine the consistency and duration of the waves: 1) The height from which the rock was dropped; 2) The weight of the rock; 3) The depth of the water.

Markets react to thrust in much the same way. Typically, a new announcement or scheduled economic report will cause this thrust in the speculative markets. Currently, the financial markets respond to Gross National Product, employment data, both the Producer Price Index and Consumer Price Index, plus many others. Veteran traders remember vividly how the Money Supply numbers of M^1 and M^2 would shock the markets each week. Now you must search to find these economic numbers. Soon a new leader of economic fundamentals will emerge and the current leaders will take their place in the history books.

Jim Twentyman has an obsession with correct data. He has the best data I have ever seen. It is flawless! What Jim and I did was to categorize all the price swings over a five minute bar chart in all major commodities. The S&P data was done in 1985. We entered each of these into the Wang computer by hand. The computer would then search for values of the price swing and report the frequency distribution of each price swing. When the distribution is skewed you would get a Poisson distribution and your first hint of a harmonic or vibratory number. It was then apparent that the only way you could prove this theory was to look at thousands of charts to see if the premise was valid. We tested the idea and found it statistically accurate and quite useful in technical analysis.

Technicians will agree that chart analysis is tantamount to reading a road map. There is an X axis and a Y axis. Chartists depict the X axis for time and the Y axis for price. Once the coordinates are found, you know the exact spot where price and time meet. This information is not going to tell you what will happen next. Nothing can do that! What it does tell you is that a pattern may be completed at that time. The neural network I am using does just that; and harmonic numbers help with this estimation. It has categorized these patterns in time and price.

As a trader, I must decide when to enter and exit the market. This is what trading is all about. I then ask myself two questions: 1) Is the pattern and ratio signal present? and 2) Can I afford to take the risk? If the answer to both of these questions is "yes," then I must take the trade. No one can tell which trades will be successful. This is a game of probabilities, but the odds and payoffs are on my side.

The only way you can use harmonic numbers is to go through example after example yourself and see how they work. It is not necessary to know why they work—they just work! Revealing something as important as those numbers used to be of concern to me. Jim Twentyman put my mind at ease with this original quote: *Defy human nature—do the work yourself!* That sums it up! Most traders want the work done for them. Is it laziness, lack of commitment or desire? I really don't know. What I do know is that only 10-15 percent of those reading this book will actually go forward and study intraday charts to prove the value of Harmonic Numbers.

The harmonic numbers illustrated here are ones that I am sure work. (There is a big clue on how to find vibratory numbers if you are interested and I'll give you that clue if you call me in Tucson, Arizona: 520/529-0469.)

Order from chaos in the Fibonacci Summation series?

I found it helpful over the years to view any market as a vibration from some energy point. What happened leaves clues to the future of price movements. The Fibonacci Summation Series is related to chaos theory. Within the chaos of market action are identifiable patterns that repeat with great frequency. One of the unusual properties of the Fibonacci series can be illustrated by the following example: take any two numbers from 1 to infinity. Any two numbers will work, but I will start with 124 and 963. Notice what happens when you do the following: add the sum of

$$
\begin{array}{rll}
 & & 124 \\
 & + & 963 \\
\hline
1 & & 1087 \\
 & + & 963 \\
\hline
2 & = & 2050 \\
 & + & 1087 \\
\hline
3 & = & 3137 \\
 & + & 2050 \\
\hline
4 & = & 5187 \\
 & + & 3137 \\
\hline
5 & = & 8324 \\
 & + & 5187 \\
\hline
6 & = & 13{,}511 \\
 & + & 8324 \\
\hline
7 & = & 21{,}835 \\
 & + & 13{,}511 \\
\hline
8 & = & 35{,}346 \\
\end{array}
$$

When you divide the seventh harmonic vibration by the eighth harmonic vibration you get the number .618 (21,835÷ 35,346 = .618). Once the eighth harmonic is reached there will be virtually no change in the ratio of the numbers as you approach infinity. This is a good ex-

ample of how two random numbers can be related in the future. Price and time patterns show the same characteristics when they repeat.

S&P—The S&P 500 has a total of five harmonic numbers; three primary and two secondary numbers. Secondary harmonic numbers are important in strongly trending markets. Primary harmonic numbers are: *270*, *350*, *540*. Secondary harmonic numbers are: *170*, *110*.

Treasury Bonds—Treasury Bonds have a harmonic number of *20*. When Treasury Bonds exceed 20 ßticks they will most often proceed to 40 ticks. In strongly trending markets, multiples of the tick harmonic should be expected (i.e., 2x20, 3x20, 4x20).

Dow Jones Industrials—The Dow Jones Industrials have a total of three harmonic numbers: two primary (*35* and *105*) and one secondary (*70*).

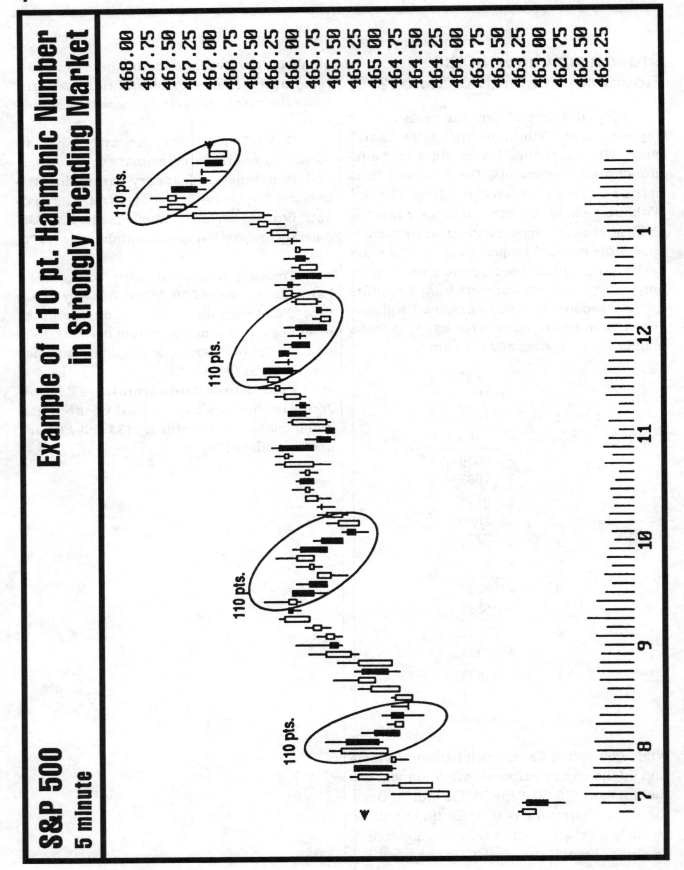

S&P 500
5 minute

Example of 110 pt. Harmonic Number in Strongly Trending Market

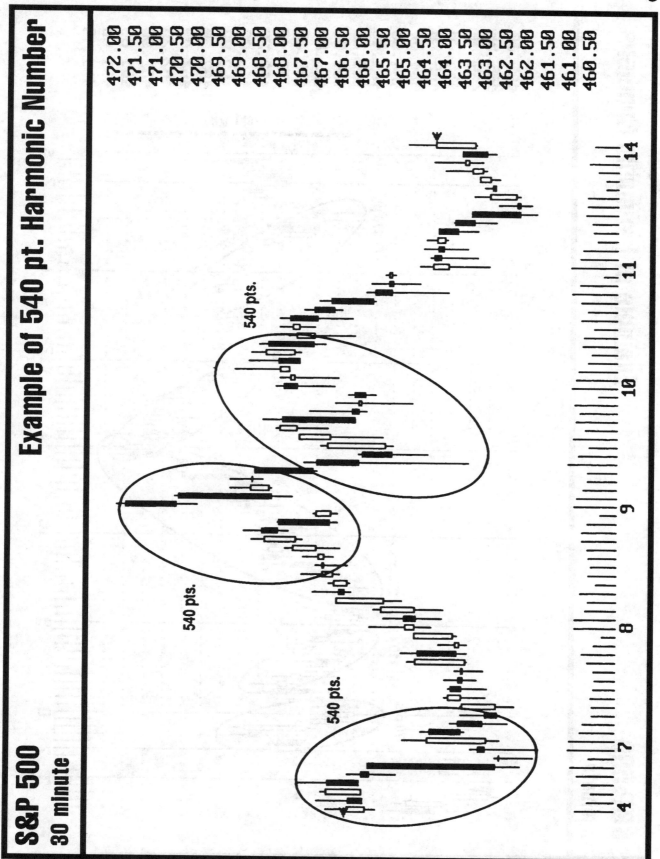

Example of 540 pt. Harmonic Number

S&P 500
30 minute

472.00
471.50
471.00
470.50
470.00
469.50
469.00
468.50
468.00
467.50
467.00
466.50
466.00
465.50
465.00
464.50
464.00
463.50
463.00
462.50
462.00
461.50
461.00
460.50

540 pts.

540 pts.

540 pts.

4　7　8　9　10　11　14

Example of Harmonic Numbers

S&P 500
5 minute

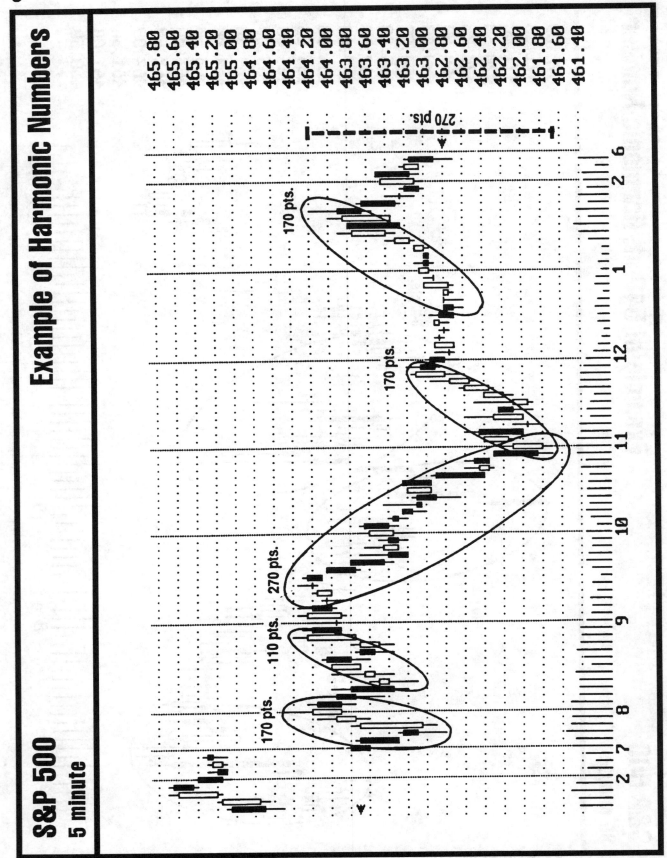

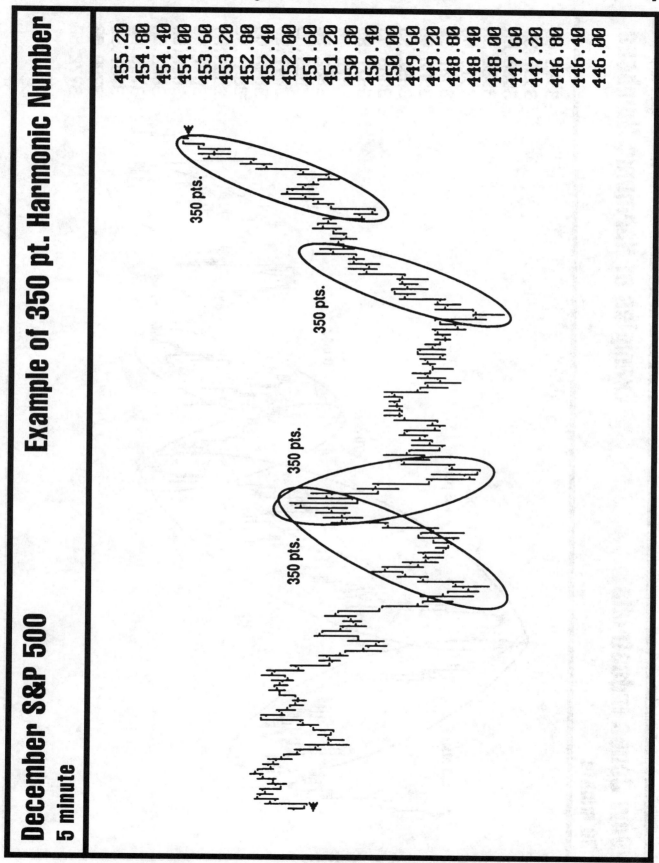

December S&P 500
5 minute

Example of 350 pt. Harmonic Number

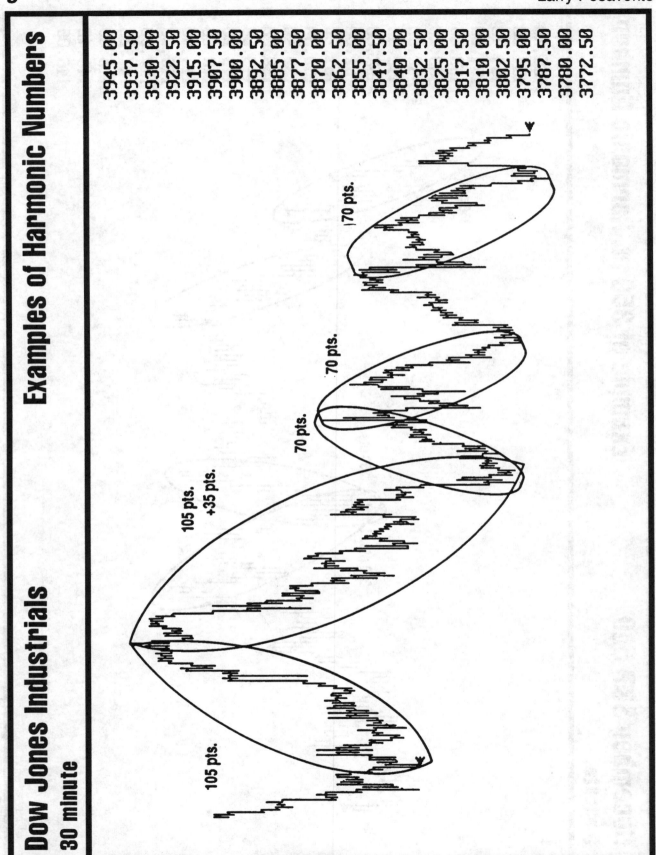

Dow Jones Industrials
30 minute

Examples of Harmonic Numbers

3945.00
3937.50
3930.00
3922.50
3915.00
3907.50
3900.00
3892.50
3885.00
3877.50
3870.00
3862.50
3855.00
3847.50
3840.00
3832.50
3825.00
3817.50
3810.00
3802.50
3795.00
3787.50
3780.00
3772.50

105 pts.

105 pts.
+35 pts.

70 pts.

70 pts.

70 pts.

70 pts.

Pfizer (PFE)
60 minute

Example of Harmonic Numbers

Notice the harmonic number (swing) in PFE. Seven point swings are occurring every several days. This information is useful to the trader for entry and exits.

122 ⊕
121 ⊕
120 ⊕
119 ⊕
118 ⊕
117 ⊕
116 ⊕
115 ⊕
114 ⊕
113 ⊕
112 ⊕
111 ⊕
110 ⊕
109 ⊕
108 ⊕
107 ⊕
106 ⊕
105 ⊕
104 ⊕
103 ⊕
102 ⊕
101 ⊕
100 ⊕
99 ⊕

Excite (XCIT)
4 minute

Example of Harmonic Numbers

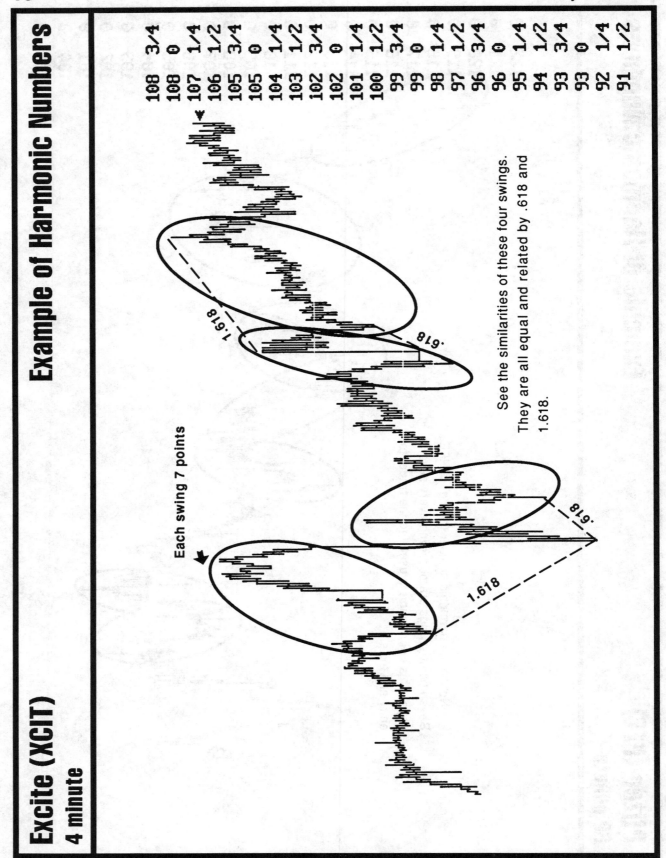

Each swing 7 points

See the similarities of these four swings.
They are all equal and related by .618 and 1.618.

108	3/4
108	0
107	1/4
106	1/2
105	3/4
105	0
104	1/4
103	1/2
102	3/4
102	0
101	1/4
100	1/2
99	3/4
99	0
98	1/4
97	1/2
96	3/4
96	0
95	1/4
94	1/2
93	3/4
93	0
92	1/4
91	1/2

Proportions of Importance
Sacred Ratios from 1-5

Ratio	Source	Reciprocal
1.000	$= \sqrt{1}$	$= 1.000$
1.272	$= \sqrt{1.618}$	$= 0.786$
1.4142	$= \sqrt{2}$	$= 0.707$
1.618	$= \phi$	$= 0.618$
1.732	$= \sqrt{3}$	$= 0.577$
1.902	$= \sqrt{(\phi^2 = 1^2)}$	$= 0.526$
2.000	$= \sqrt{4}$	$= 0.500$
2.236	$= \sqrt{5} \ \& \ \phi + 1/\phi$	$= 0.447$
3.000	$= \sqrt{9} \ \& \ \phi^2 + 1/\phi^2$	$= 0.333$
3.142	$= \pi$	$= 0.318$
4.000	$= 2^2$	$= 0.25$
5.000	$= 2 + 3$	$= 0.20$

These ratios are not "sacred" in the religious sense, but they are sacred to the study of geometry. Just about every price swing imaginable can be found using one of these ratios. *For trading the patterns I use, you only need to look for five ratios: .618, .786, 1.00, 1.27 and 1.618.*

It can be very helpful to know the market you are following is vibratory to .707 or 1.414 instead of the .618 or 1.618.

Finding out why the market did not make one of five ratios can be very important in determining what it is going to do next. The following charts are examples of $\sqrt{2}$ and $1/\sqrt{2}$.

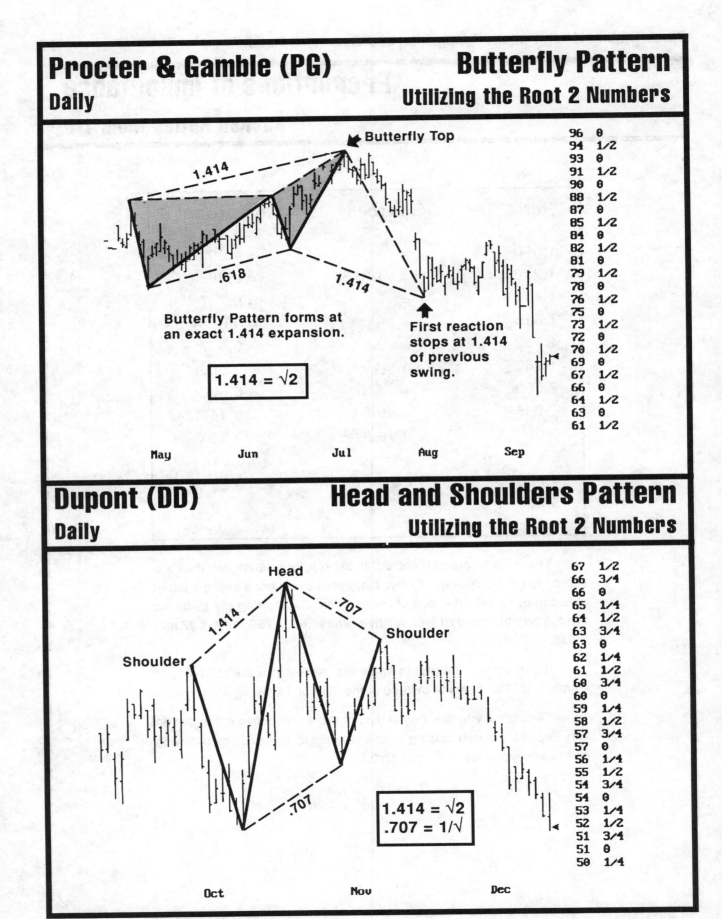

Procter & Gamble (PG)
Daily

Butterfly Pattern
Utilizing the Root 2 Numbers

Butterfly Top

1.414

.618

1.414

Butterfly Pattern forms at
an exact 1.414 expansion.

First reaction
stops at 1.414
of previous
swing.

$$1.414 = \sqrt{2}$$

96	0
94	1/2
93	0
91	1/2
90	0
88	1/2
87	0
85	1/2
84	0
82	1/2
81	0
79	1/2
78	0
76	1/2
75	0
73	1/2
72	0
70	1/2
69	0
67	1/2
66	0
64	1/2
63	0
61	1/2

May   Jun   Jul   Aug   Sep

Dupont (DD)
Daily

Head and Shoulders Pattern
Utilizing the Root 2 Numbers

Head

1.414

.707

Shoulder

Shoulder

.707

$$1.414 = \sqrt{2}$$
$$.707 = 1/\sqrt{}$$

67	1/2
66	3/4
66	0
65	1/4
64	1/2
63	3/4
63	0
62	1/4
61	1/2
60	3/4
60	0
59	1/4
58	1/2
57	3/4
57	0
56	1/4
55	1/2
54	3/4
54	0
53	1/4
52	1/2
51	3/4
51	0
50	1/4

Oct   Nov   Dec

The Geometric Characteristics of a Price Chart

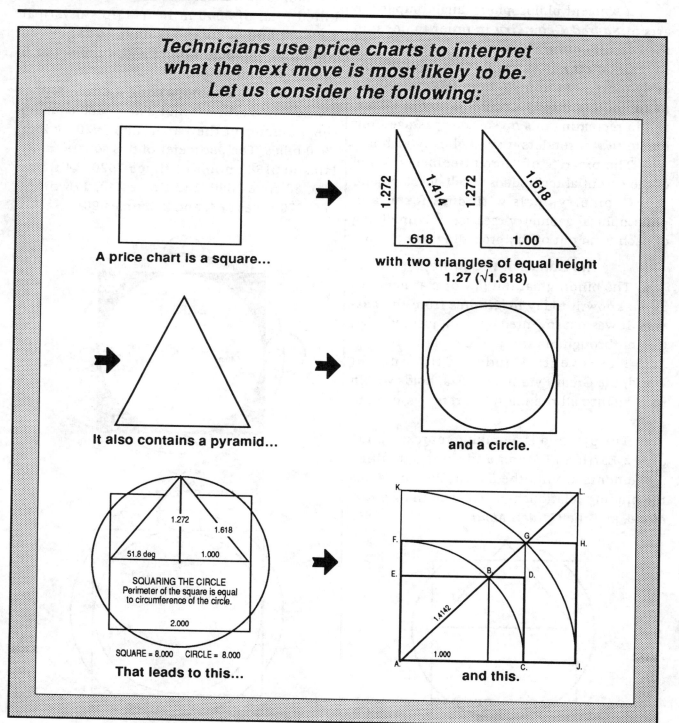

Technicians use price charts to interpret
what the next move is most likely to be.
Let us consider the following:

A price chart is a square...

**with two triangles of equal height
1.27 (√1.618)**

1.272 1.414 .618

1.272 1.618 1.00

It also contains a pyramid...

and a circle.

1.272 1.618
51.8 deg 1.000

SQUARING THE CIRCLE
Perimeter of the square is equal
to circumference of the circle.

2.000

SQUARE = 8.000   CIRCLE = 8.000

That leads to this...

K L
F. G H.
E. B D.
1.4142
A. 1.000 C. J.

and this.

Geometric Principles
by Bryce Gilmore

Philosophical Geometry

Ancient philosophers taught pupils the arts of **Sacred Geometry** in order to develop their faculty of **intuition**.

Geometry attempts to recapture the orderly movement from an infinite formlessness to an endless interconnected array of forms, and in recreating this mysterious passage from **one** to **two**, it renders it symbolically viable.

The practice of Sacred Geometry is one of the essential techniques of self-development.

Geometry deals with pure form, and philosophical geometry reenacts the unfolding of each form out of the preceding one.

The Canon of Proportion

The binding natural law of mathematics as we know it today **originates** from the **cosmos**. It was not invented by man, just revealed to him through his study of the planets.

The Seventh Wonder of the Ancient World, the Great Pyramid of Giza, holds within its structure all the math "secrets" we need to know.

The pyramid is a graphic representation of the Earth and Moon and their combined movements around the Sun. It demonstrates the binding relationships between the **square**, **circle**, and the **Golden Mean**.

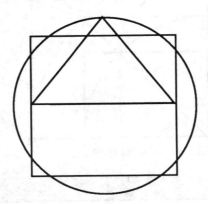

Modern day scientific studies have (among other things) confirmed the measurements of the Moon and the Earth.

The radius of the Moon is 1090 miles and the radius of the Earth is 3960 miles. A combined total of 5040 miles (Plato's mystical number and in calendar days equal to 720 weeks, 2 times 360, 3 times 240, 4 times 180, 5 times 144, and 8 times 90).

A square encompassing a circle representing the Earth has four sides, each equal to the diameter of the Earth, i.e., 3920 by 2 or 7920 miles. The perimeter of this square calculates to 31680 miles (4 times 7920, 44 times 720, 88 times 360, 132 times 240, 176 times 180, 220 times 144, and 352 times 90).

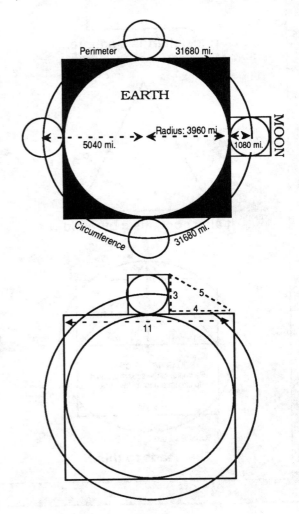

If the Moon and the Earth were placed side by side (see illustration on previous page), the distance between the two centers would be equal to the sum of the radii, i.e., 3920 plus 1080, which equals 5040 miles. A circle drawn using the combined radii of 5040 would have a circumference of 2 π r or 2 x 22/7 x 5040, which equals 31680.

The relationship of the circle's circumference to the square's perimeter is 1.000:1.000. This geometric exercise is known as squaring the circle. Pi is the Pythagorean measure of 22/7 used to calculate the dimensions in a circle or sphere. In decimal form Pi is the irrational number 3.14159.

The radius of the circle 5040 (1080 + 3960) as a factor of the Earth's radius is equal to 5040:3960 or 1.2727:1.000. And 1.272 is mathematically the square root of 1.618.

Squaring the Circle

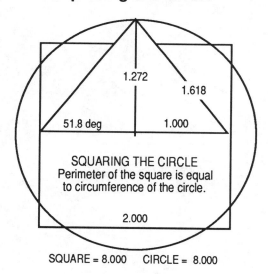

SQUARING THE CIRCLE
Perimeter of the square is equal
to circumference of the circle.

SQUARE = 8.000   CIRCLE = 8.000

A hypotenuse calculation for a right-angled triangle using the 5040 radius of the above circle and half the side of the above square, i.e., the radius of the Earth 3960, would give the following result.

Using the Pythagorean theorem, i.e., the length of the hypotenuse in a right triangle (90 degree triangle) will be equal to the square root of the sum of the squares of the other two sides.

Hypotenuse = square root [(5040 x 5040) + (3960 x 3960)] = 6409 miles.

If we call the base of the triangle the Earth's radius, i.e., 3960, then the hypotenuse 6409.6 as a ratio of the base 3960 is 6409:3960 or 1.618:1.000.

The irrational number 1.272 is the square root of 1.618, i.e., 1.272 = $\sqrt{1.618}$.

It can be demonstrated by this exercise where the designers of the Great Pyramid of Giza procured their measurements. It can also be seen that the irrational numbers of φ = 1.618 and π = 3.14159 are related.

1/4 (3.142) = 0.786 (1/√.618)

1/4 is the harmonic ratio from the square and 1.618 is the Golden Mean.

Harmonic Ratios from the Square
The Diagonal of the Square
(Root 2 = 1.4142)

The square is bounded by four equal sides at right angles to each other.

Using the Pythagorean theorem we can calculate the diagonal length. This number will always maintain the same relationship to any side of the square (1.4142:1).

A square with sides equal to 1.000 has a diagonal of: $\sqrt{(1^2 + 1^2)}$ or $\sqrt{2}$, which is 1.4142.

The diagonal of any square relates as 1.4142:1.000 with its side.

Expanding a square by the ratio of its diagonal produces the Harmonic Ratio Series.

1.000   1.4142   2.000   2.828

The inverse ratio relationships are:

0.354   0.500   0.707   1.000

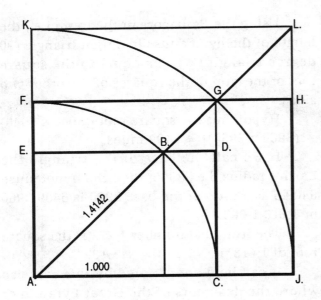

1.618 is commonly known as the Golden Mean, is represented by the Greek symbol Φ and is called PHI.

If we call the height of the triangle the combined radii of the Earth and Moon, i.e., 3960 + 1080 or 5040, then the hypotenuse 6409 as a ratio of the height is 6409:5040 or 1.272:1.000.

Those of you who would like to explore the many complexities of the geometry of markets should get Bruce Gilmore's book *Geometry of Markets* and Robert Miner's *Dynamic Trader*.

Example of Ratios of Proportion

Cash S&P 500
4 minute

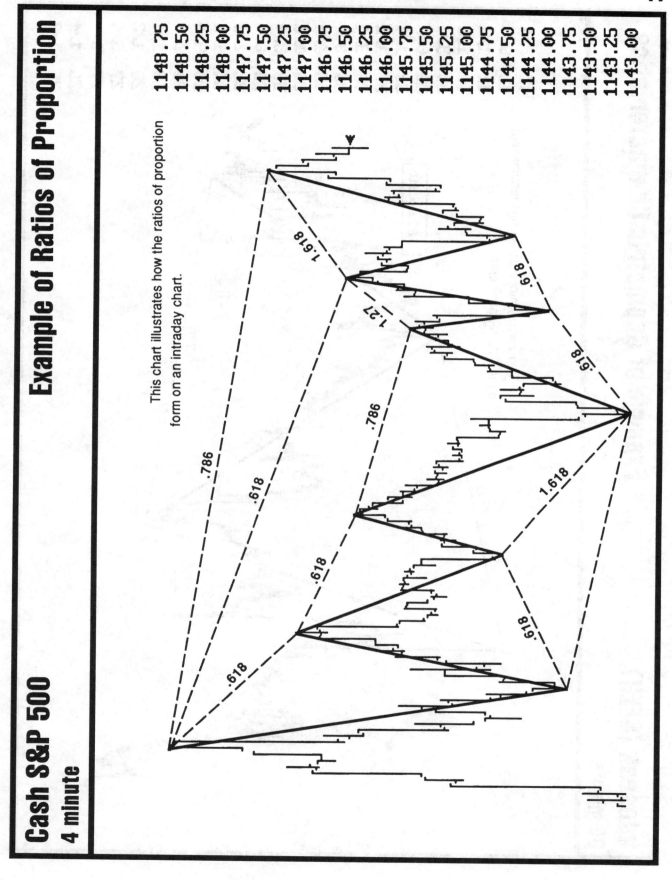

This chart illustrates how the ratios of proportion form on an intraday chart.

Example of Geometric Characteristics

Infoseek (SEEK)
30 minute

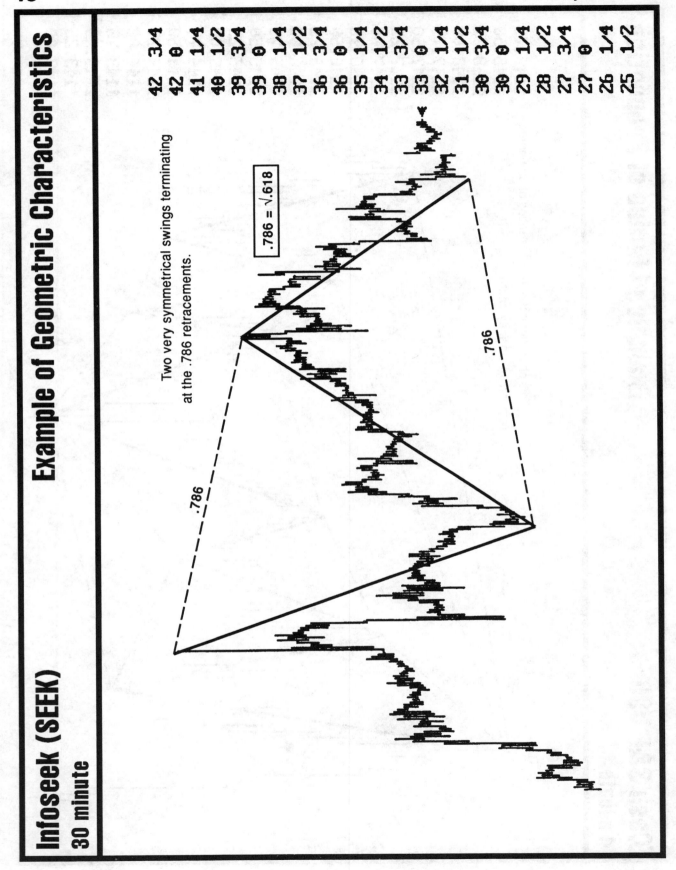

Two very symmetrical swings terminating

at the .786 retracements.

.786 = √.618

.786

.786

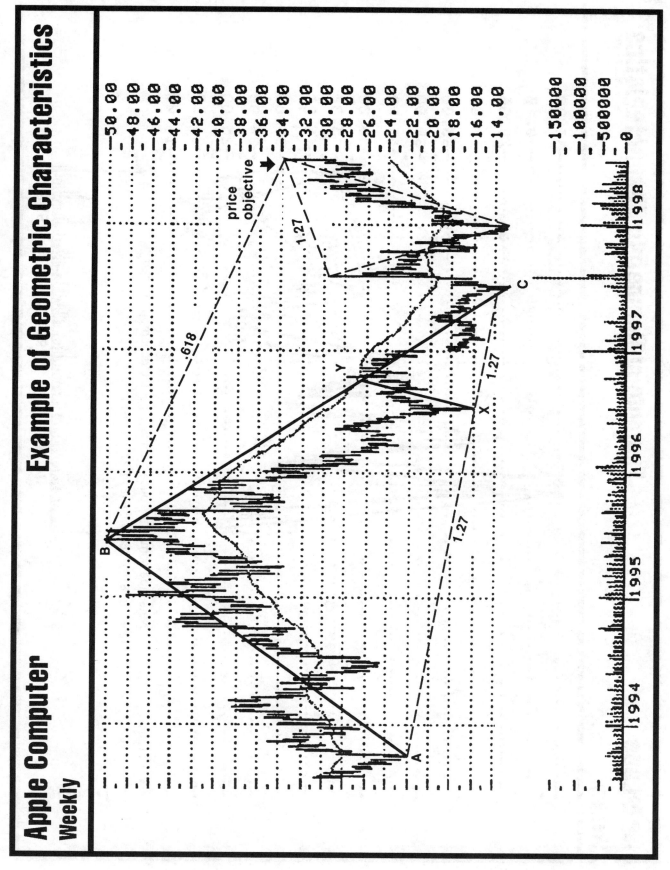

Apple Computer
Weekly

Example of Geometric Characteristics

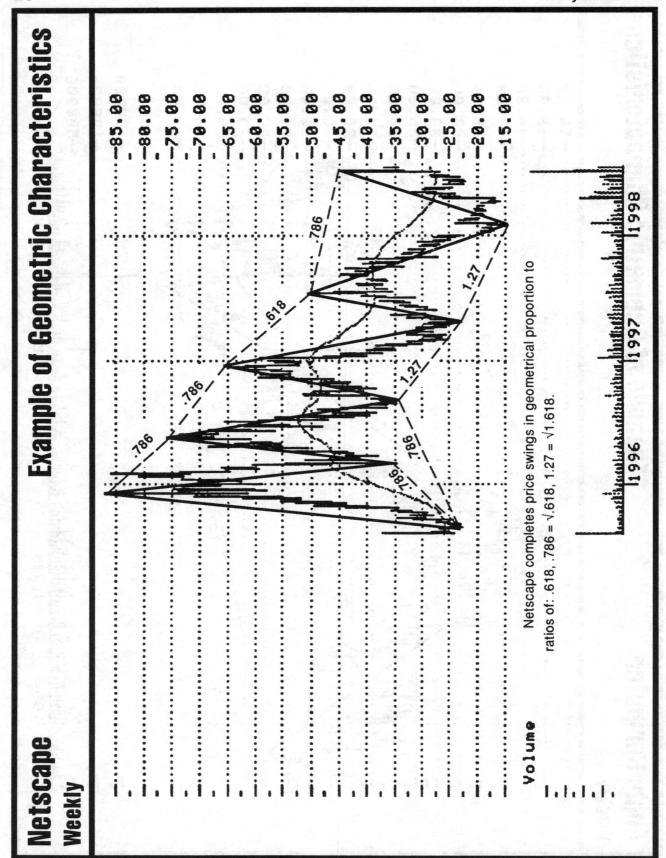

Example of Geometric Characteristics

Netscape
Weekly

Netscape completes price swings in geometrical proportion to ratios of: .618, .786 = √.618, 1.27 = √1.618.

The Primary Patterns

This section discusses the primary patterns I use in trading. Many of my students ask me why I share this information. It is quite simple and has a two part answer. First, all of these patterns were found by someone else over the past 70 years. Second, every trader has his own time frame that he likes to trade, so the chance of a self-fulling trade expectation is very remote.

One very important difference will emerge from this section on pattern recognition. That difference is that *all* of the patterns discussed will be illustrated using the mathematical ratios of ancient geometry, of which the Fibonacci Summation series is a part. What I tried to do is show how you can use only four numbers of the Fibonacci Summation series to mathematically identify these patterns. I always thought that the mathematical relationship of these price swings is what the originators of these patterns failed to bring up. This is especially true for the Elliott Wave theoreticians. I studied the Elliott Wave principle extensively from 1974 to 1978. I thought his tenets on wave patterns were more like guidelines than immutable laws. To this day, if you get 12 Elliott Wave theorists in a room you will end up with 24 or more interpretations of the price action. There is nothing wrong with that. It is just another way of showing that no one knows what is going to happen next in the markets. More importantly it also reitierates that it is not necessary to know what is going to happen next. What is necessary is to *know the risk* on the trade. Since we are dealing with mathematical relationships, the control of risk can be quantified easily.

I spent the better part of 30 years looking at these patterns. My sources originated from Don Mack at the Investment Center in Santa Monica, California and John Hill at the Commodity Research Institute in Hendersonville, North Carolina. I do not think I overlooked anyone who ever described a price pattern. There are two books that I highly recommend:

1. *Profits in the Stock Market* by H.M. Gartley (1935). This was Gartley's Stock Market course in the 1930s. It cost $1500 which was equivalent to 3 Ford automobiles at the time. On pages 200 to 250 most of the patterns ever discussed are found. More trading systems were rediscovered and sold from this book than any other book. This includes: The Tubbs Stock Market Course, The Trident Strategy, The Reversal Point Wave, and many others. The book is more than 700 pages and comes with huge wall charts illustrating the action of the stock market in the 1920's and 1930s. It can be purchased for under $100 from Traders Press in Greenville, SC, 800-927-8222.

2. *Torque Analysis of Stock Market Cycles* by William Garrett (1971). This book is a true gem. It was the first book ever written that explores the mathematical and geometrical relationships of price patterns and how they relate to the numbers of ancient geometry. Garrett's book came out at about the same time as another book on cycles. James Hurst's *The Profit Magic of Stock Transaction Timing*. Hurst's book was less expensive and much easier to read. But the content of Garrett's book held the key to many answers about cycles and Fibonacci numbers. Only 200 copies of Garrett's book were ever sold. Prentice Hall destroyed the remainder of copies due to the need for warehouse space.

If you spend some time looking through my bibliography, you will see that a great number of authors are covered. I always felt that each of them contributed to the science of technical studies.

The Ten Basic Patterns

Pattern One

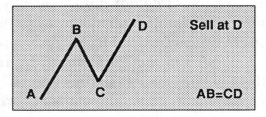

Pattern Two

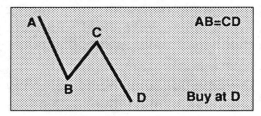

Patterns One and Two were first described on page 249 of H. M. Gartley's *Profits in the Stock Market* (see the original illustration below). It is the basic pattern in the theory of parallel channels. From this one page in Gartley's book, two of the most famous trading systems were sold. The first was the Tubbs Stock Market course ($1500 in the 1950s) and The Trident Strategy ($3000 in 1970s).

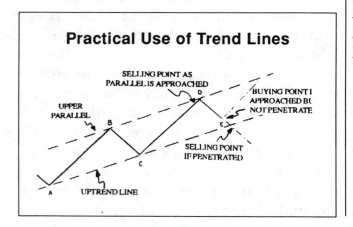

Pattern Three
Gartley "222"

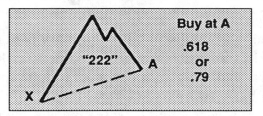

Pattern Four
Gartley "222"

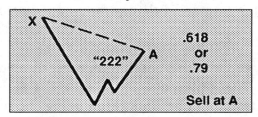

The Gartley "222" Pattern (illustrated in Patterns Three and Four) is one of the best I have ever found. I named it the Gartley "222" pattern because it is on page 222 in Gartley's book. He spent more time describing this pattern than all the others. This pattern shows why it is not necessary to pick a top or bottom—just wait for the first "222" pattern following the top or bottom. The real beauty of it is that it contains an AB=CD pattern within it. This allows the trader to calculate ratio and proportions of various price waves in order to determine the risk on the trade. If the day trader learns only this pattern he will do very well. It is worth noting that when the "222" pattern fails (market moves beyond point X) a major continuation move is in progress.

Pattern Five

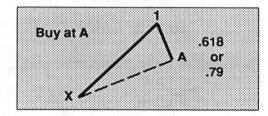

Pattern Six

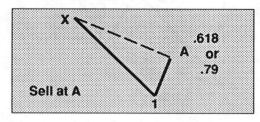

Pattern Seven

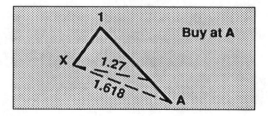

Pattern Eight

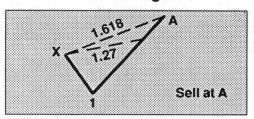

Patterns Five and Six are reaction patterns. The move from point 1 can be 38%, 50%, 61%, 70.7%, 78%, 100% (double top or bottom). The only time I use the 38% retracement level to find a trade entry is when the move from X to 1 is one of tremendous thrust (three to five times normal trading range bars). The market will give you strong clues as to what it will do next if you watch the retracements in new moves. If it reacts only 38% on the first reaction swing, then a high probability exists that the next swing or two will also be 38% reactions.

Patterns Seven and Eight are extension patterns. It was this pattern that changed my approach to trading. As I was trading from Switzerland, where I had spoken to a group of Swiss bankers, almost every trade I put on over the last several days had been stopped out on a penetration of point X. In my hotel room, I was calculating why my stop was right at the high/low of the day. I had placed my stop right at the 1.27 move of X to 1. It was upon hitting the square root button on my calculator that I first began to see the importance of the 1.27 ratio ($\sqrt{1.618} = 1.27$).

A good rule of thumb is to wait for a candlestick pattern such as a *doji* or *hammer* (page 97) when point A is reached. Remember that this pattern is an extension pattern and there are no guarantees that the swing cannot go much higher.

Pattern Nine

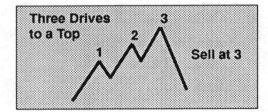

Pattern Ten

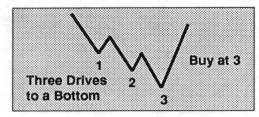

Patterns Nine and Ten are the most diffi-cult to find on daily charts. They are found more frequently on intraday charts (5 minute, 30 minute, etc.). William Dunnigan described this pattern in *Dunnigan's One-Way Method* and the *Dunnigan Thrust Method*. The three drive pattern should be very esthetic to the eyes of the trader. It should jump out at you. If you find that you are forcing the pattern to fit three drives, it is probably not correct. The most important thing to keep in mind is sym-metry: The waves should be symmetrical in price and time. *(Note: In her book* Street Smarts, *Linda Bradford Raschke refers to this pattern as the* Three Little Indians.*)*

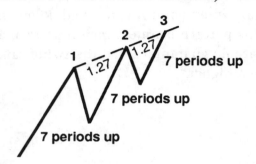

The diagram above is an example only. It shows the number of periods could be 3 to 13. The price swing could also be 1.618.

Characteristics of Patterns

Pattern One

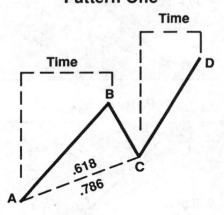

1. Price swing from A to B will be equal to CD 60 percent of the time. The other 40 per-cent of the time CD will be 1.27 or 1.618 of AB.

2. The BC swing will be .618 or .786 of the AB move. In very strongly trending markets the BC swing will only be at the .382 retracement.

3. If the AB swing is very strong, it will give a good clue what to expect on the BC move.

4. The time bars from point A to B should be equal to the CD time bars about 60 per-cent of the time. The other 40 percent of the time these time periods will expand to 1.27 or 1.618 of AB.

5. Should the CD price swing have a price gap or a very wide range bar, the trader should interpret this as a sign of extreme strength and expect to see price expan-sions of 1.27 or 1.618.

Example of Primary Pattern One

December S&P
60 minute

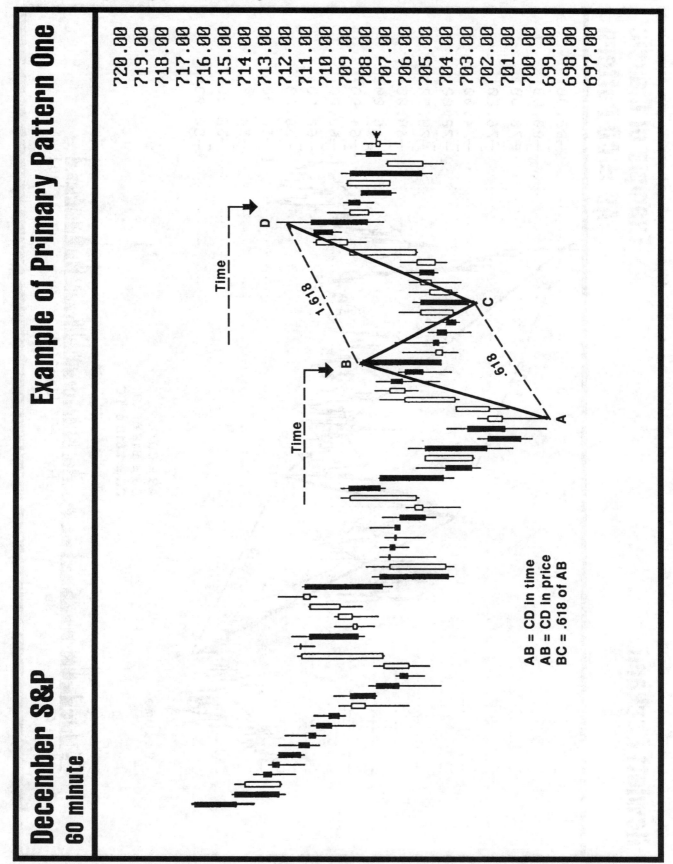

720.00
719.00
718.00
717.00
716.00
715.00
714.00
713.00
712.00
711.00
710.00
709.00
708.00
707.00
706.00
705.00
704.00
703.00
702.00
701.00
700.00
699.00
698.00
697.00

AB = CD in time
AB = CD in price
BC = .618 of AB

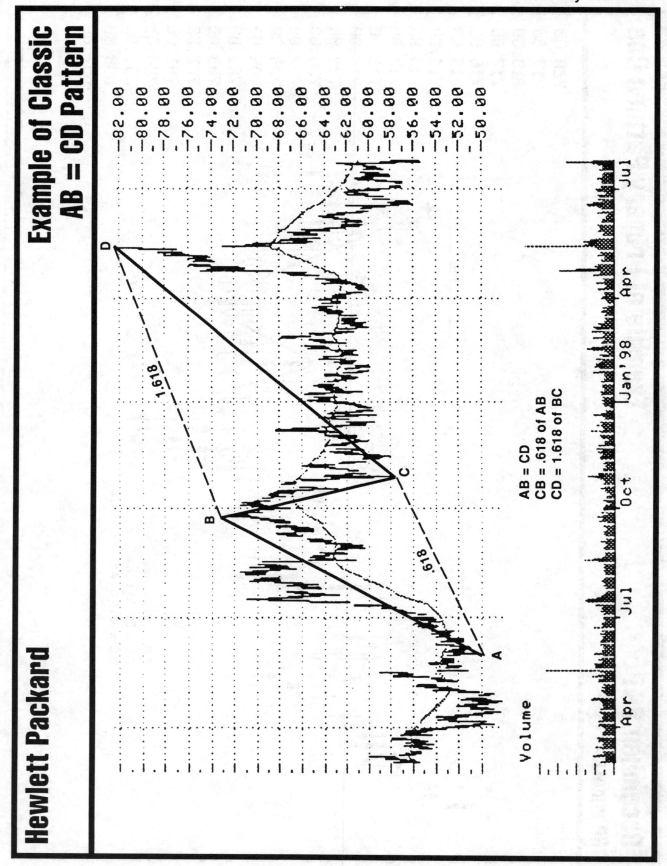

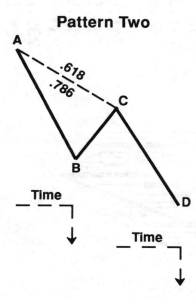

Pattern Two

1. Price swing from A to B will be equal to CD 60 percent of the time. The other 40 percent of the time CD will be 1.27 or 1.618 of AB.

2. The BC swing will be .618 or .786 of the AB move. In very strongly trending markets the BC swing will only be at the .382 retracement.

3. If the AB swing is very strong, it will give a good clue what to expect on the BC move.

4. The time bars from point A to B should be equal to the CD time bars about 60 percent of the time. The other 40 percent of the time these time periods will expand to 1.27 or 1.618 of AB.

5. Should the CD price swing have a price gap or a very wide range bar, the trader should interpret this as a sign of extreme strength and expect to see price expansions of 1.27 or 1.618.

December S&P 500

Example of Primary Pattern Two

749.00
748.50
748.00
747.50
747.00
746.50
746.00
745.50
745.00
744.50
744.00
743.50
743.00
742.50
742.00
741.50
741.00
740.50
740.00
739.50
739.00
738.50
738.00
737.50

AB = CD

McDonald's Corp. (MCD) Daily

Example of Primary Pattern Two

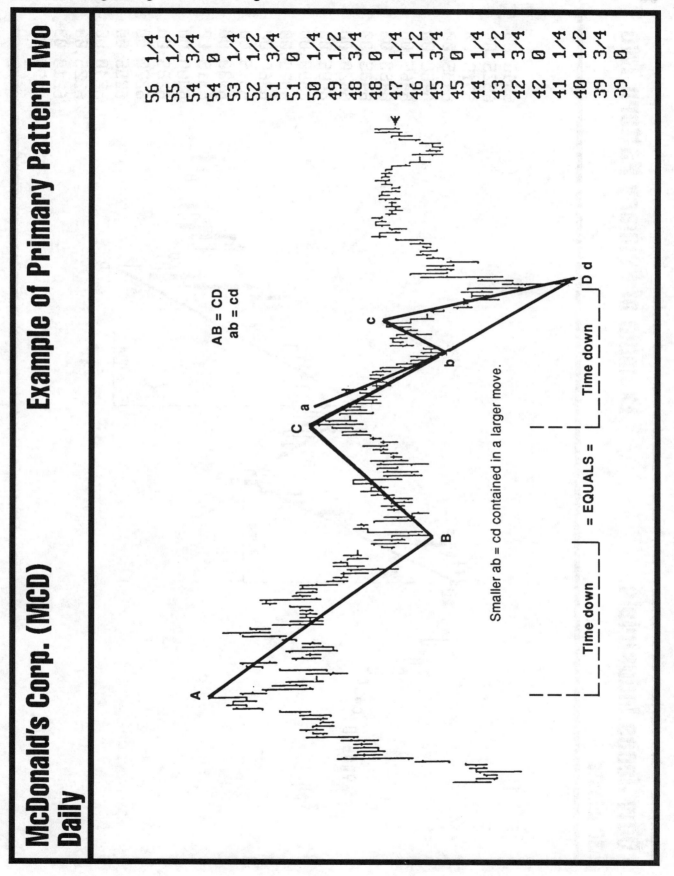

AB = CD
ab = cd

Smaller ab = cd contained in a larger move.

Time down = EQUALS = Time down

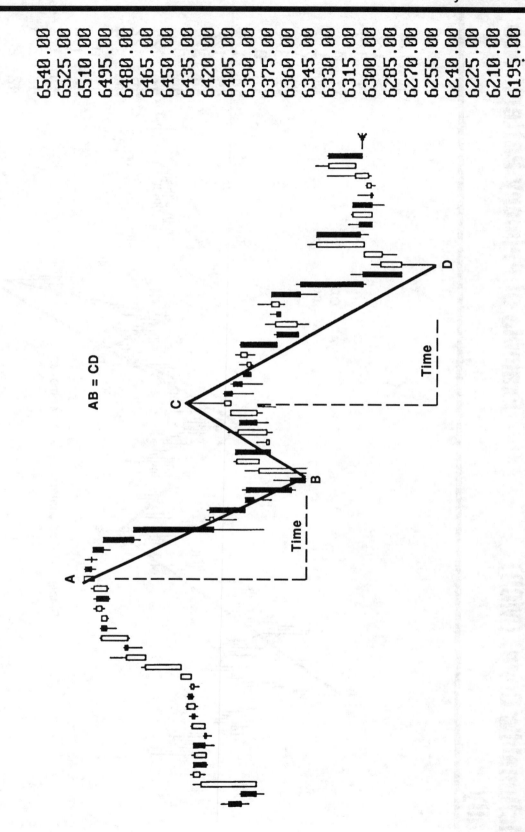

Dow Jones Industrials
30 minute

Example of Primary Pattern Two

AB = CD

December S&P 500
5 minute

Example of Primary Pattern Two

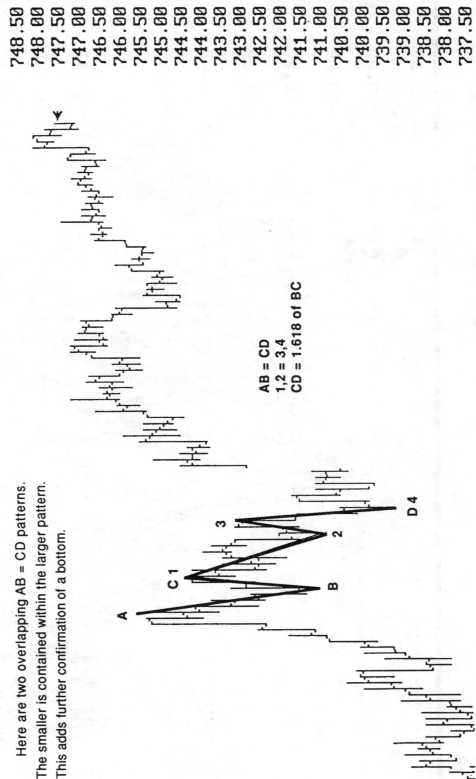

Here are two overlapping AB = CD patterns.
The smaller is contained within the larger pattern.
This adds further confirmation of a bottom.

AB = CD
1,2 = 3,4
CD = 1.618 of BC

748.50
748.00
747.50
747.00
746.50
746.00
745.50
745.00
744.50
744.00
743.50
743.00
742.50
742.00
741.50
741.00
740.50
740.00
739.50
739.00
738.50
738.00
737.50
737.00

Example of Primary Pattern Two

Motorola
Weekly

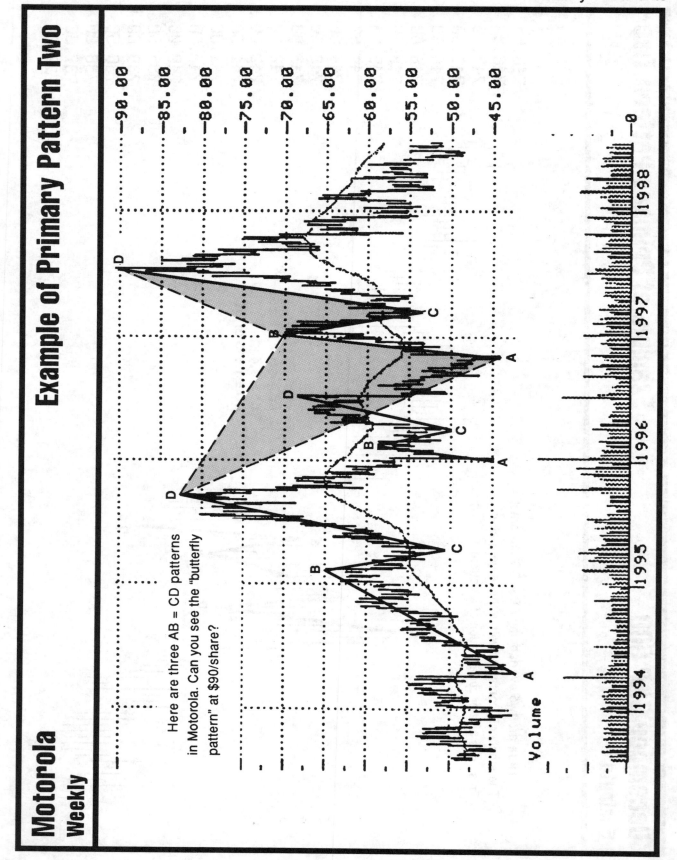

Here are three AB = CD patterns in Motorola. Can you see the "butterfly pattern" at $90/share?

Volume

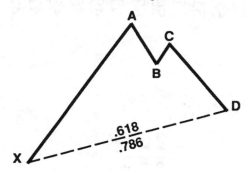

Pattern Three
Bullish Gartley "222"

1. The swing down from point A will terminate at point D. This will be at the .618 or .786 retracements 75 percent of the time. The other 25 percent of the time, the retracements will be .382, .500 or .707.

2. There must be an AB = CD pattern observed in the move from A to D.

3. The BC move will be .618 or .786 of AB. In strongly trending markets expect a .382 or .500 retracement.

4. Analyze the time frames from point X to A and A to D. These time frames will also be in ratio and proportion. For example, the number of time bars up from point X to A is equal to 17 bars. The time bars from A to D equal 11. Seventeen is approximately 1.618 of 11.

5. There will be a few instances where the AB = CD move will give a price objective at point X. This will be a true double bottom formation.

6. If point X is exceeded the trend will continue to move down to at least 1.27 or 1.618 of the X to A move.

General Motors (GM)
Daily

Example of Primary Pattern Three
Gartley "222"

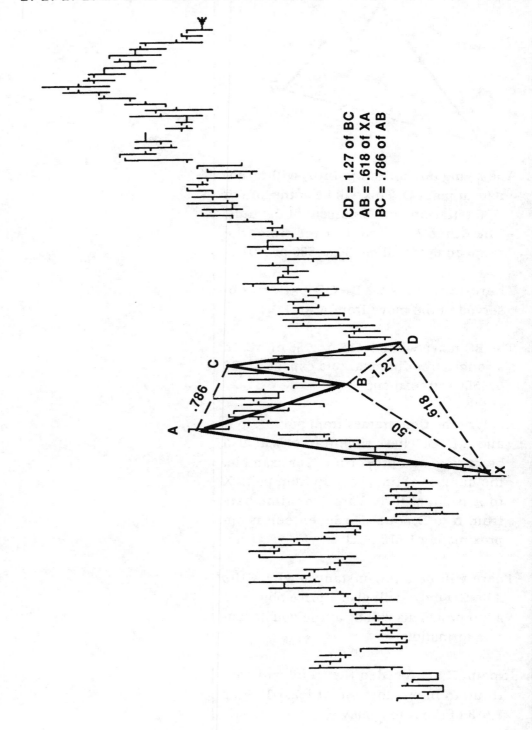

CD = 1.27 of BC
AB = .618 of XA
BC = .786 of AB

Example of Primary Pattern Three
Gartley "222"

March S&P 500
1 minute

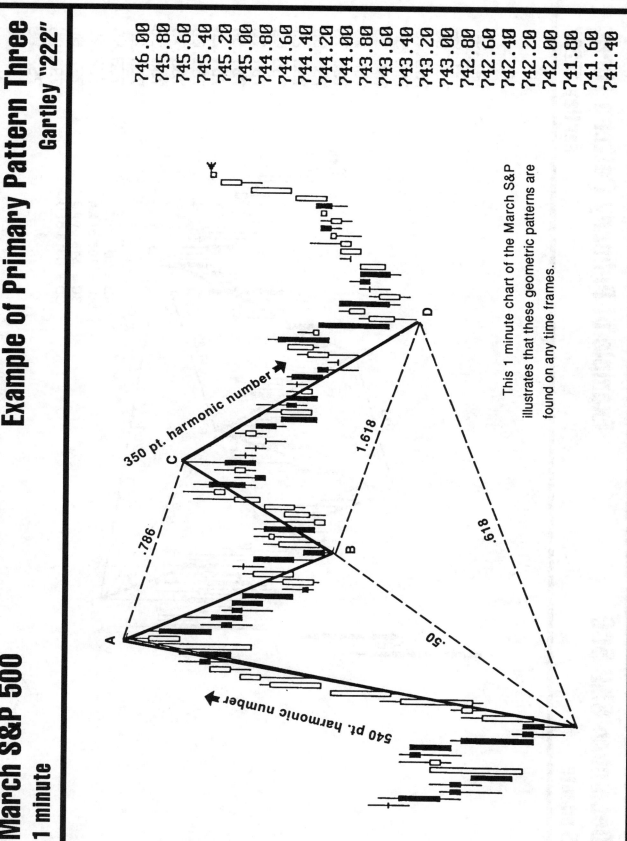

746.00
745.80
745.60
745.40
745.20
745.00
744.80
744.60
744.40
744.20
744.00
743.80
743.60
743.40
743.20
743.00
742.80
742.60
742.40
742.20
742.00
741.80
741.60
741.40

350 pt. harmonic number

540 pt. harmonic number

.786

1.618

.618

.50

A

B

C

D

This 1 minute chart of the March S&P illustrates that these geometric patterns are found on any time frames.

December S&P 500
5 minute

Example of Primary Pattern Three
Gartley "222"

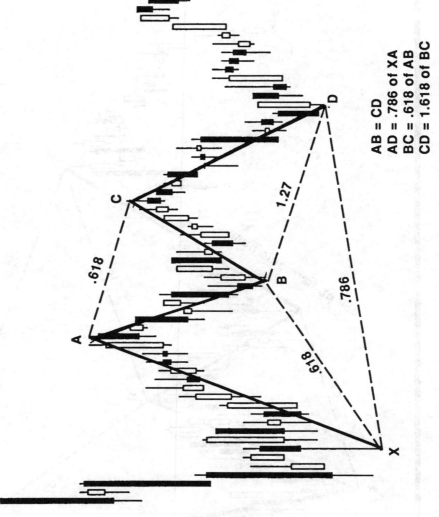

757.50
757.25
757.00
756.75
756.50
756.25
756.00
755.75
755.50
755.25
755.00
754.75
754.50
754.25
754.00
753.75
753.50
753.25
753.00
752.75
752.50
752.25
752.00
751.75

AB = CD
AD = .786 of XA
BC = .618 of AB
CD = 1.618 of BC

Dow Jones Industrials (DJI)
30 minute

Example of Primary Pattern Three
Gartley "222"

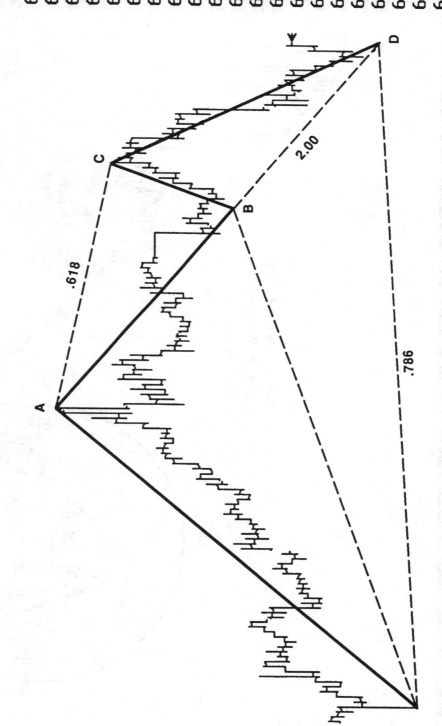

Microsoft (MSFT)
30 minute

Example of Primary Pattern Three
Gartley "222"

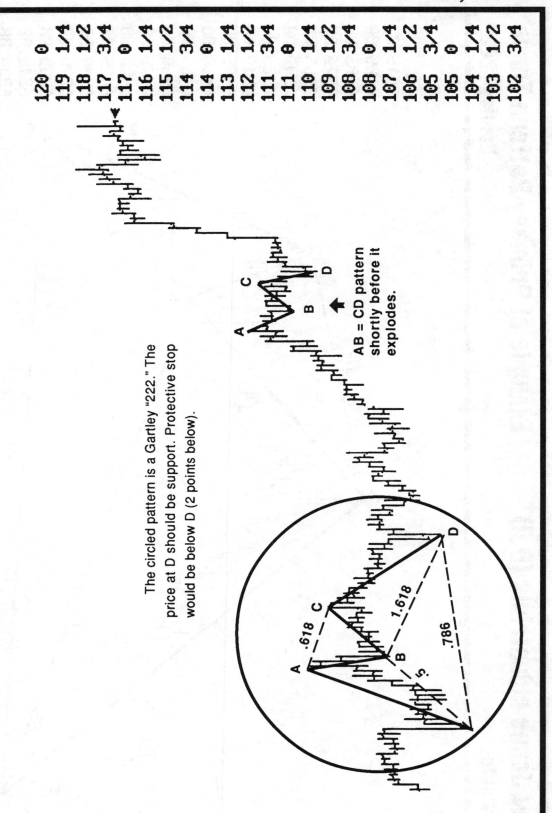

The circled pattern is a Gartley "222." The price at D should be support. Protective stop would be below D (2 points below).

AB = CD pattern shortly before it explodes.

120	0
119	1/4
118	1/2
117	3/4
117	0
116	1/4
115	1/2
114	3/4
114	0
113	1/4
112	1/2
111	3/4
111	0
110	1/4
109	1/2
108	3/4
108	0
107	1/4
106	1/2
105	3/4
105	0
104	1/4
103	1/2
102	3/4

Double Click (DCLK)
4 minute

Example of Primary Pattern Three
Gartley "222"

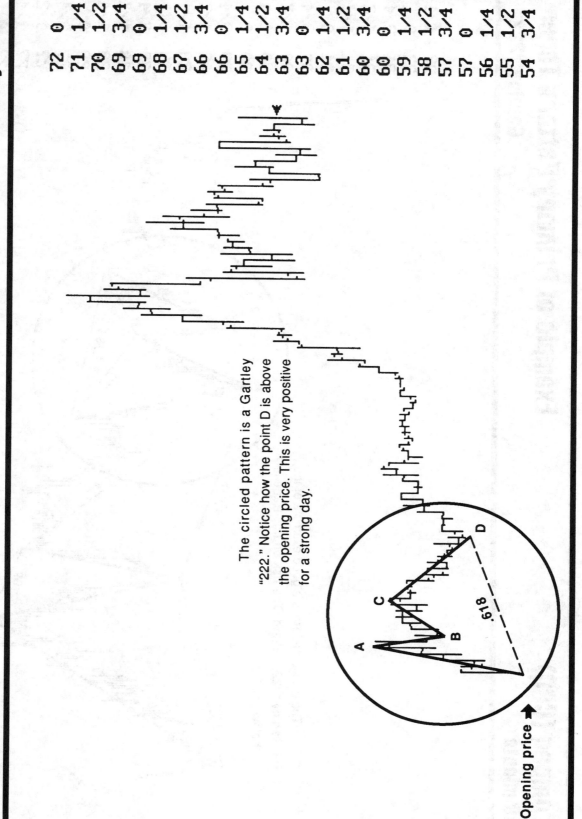

The circled pattern is a Gartley "222." Notice how the point D is above the opening price. This is very positive for a strong day.

Opening price

Example of Primary Pattern Three
Gartley "222"

Compaq (CPQ)
30 minute

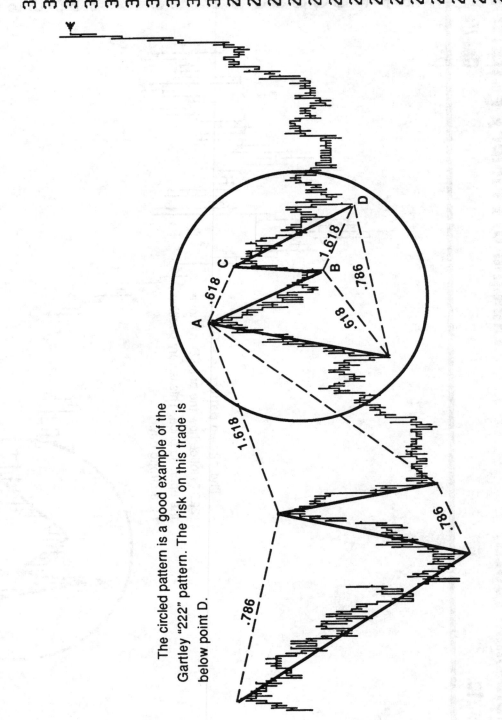

The circled pattern is a good example of the Gartley "222" pattern. The risk on this trade is below point D.

32	1/4
32	0
31	3/4
31	1/2
31	1/4
31	0
30	3/4
30	1/2
30	1/4
30	0
29	3/4
29	1/2
29	1/4
29	0
28	3/4
28	1/2
28	1/4
28	0
27	3/4
27	1/2
27	1/4
27	0
26	3/4
26	1/2

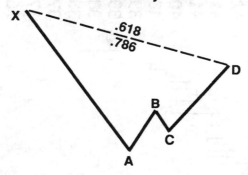

Pattern Four
Bearish Gartley "222"

1. The swing down from point A will terminate at point D. This will be at the .618 or .786 retracements 75 percent of the time. The other 25% of the time, the retracements will be .382, .500 or .707.

2. There must be an AB = CD pattern observed in the move from A to D.

3. The BC move will be .618 or .786 of AB. In strongly trending markets expect a .382 or .500 retracement.

4. Analyze the time frames from point X to A and A to D. These time frames will also be in ratio and proportion. For example, the number of time bars up from point X to A is equal to 17 bars. The time bars from A to D equal 11. Seventeen is approximately 1.618 of 11.

5. There will be a few instances where the AB = CD move will give a price objective at point X. This will be a true double bottom formation.

6. If point X is exceeded the trend will continue to move down to at least 1.27 or 1.618 of the X to A move.

General Telephone (GTE)

Example of Primary Pattern Four
Gartley "222"

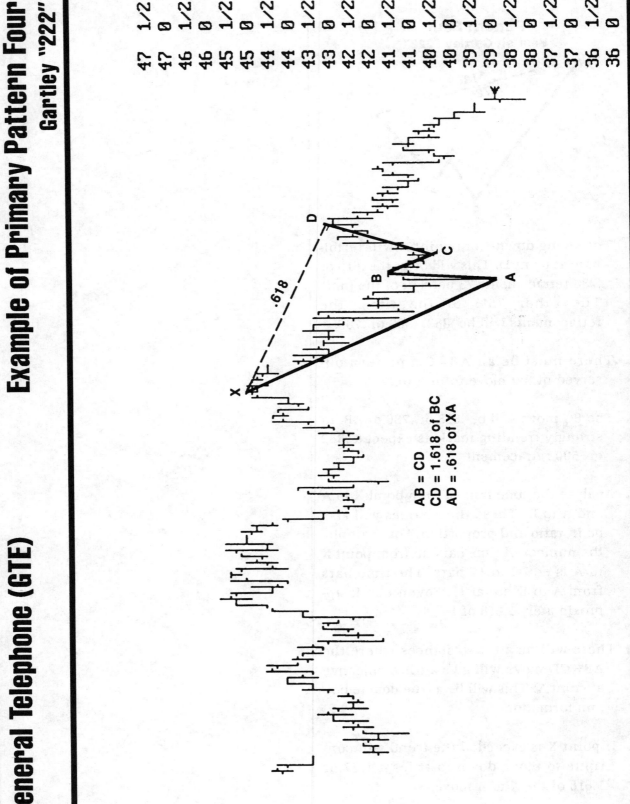

AB = CD
CD = 1.618 of BC
AD = .618 of XA

.618

American Express (AXP)
Daily

Example of Primary Pattern Four
Gartley "222"

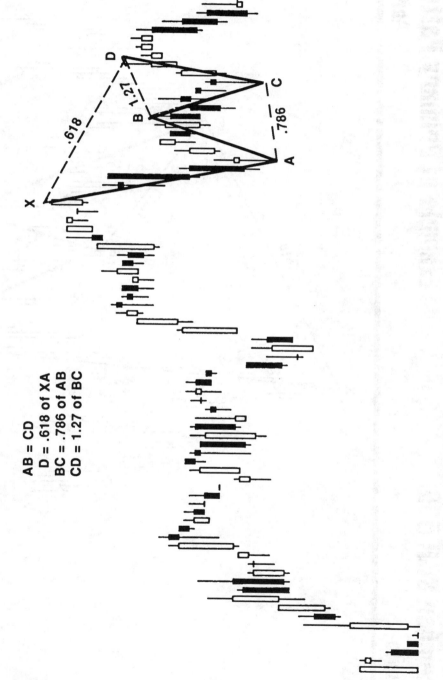

AB = CD
D = .618 of XA
BC = .786 of AB
CD = 1.27 of BC

53	0
52	1/2
52	0
51	1/2
51	0
50	1/2
50	0
49	1/2
49	0
48	1/2
48	0
47	1/2
47	0
46	1/2
46	0
45	1/2
45	0
44	1/2
44	0
43	1/2
43	0
42	1/2
42	0
41	1/2

December S&P 500

5 minute

Example of Primary Pattern Four

Gartley "222"

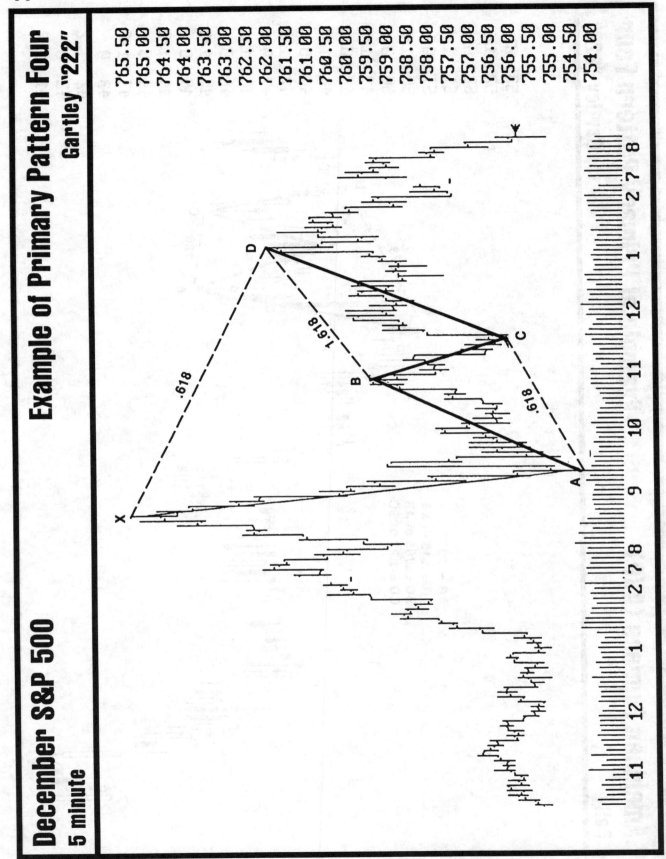

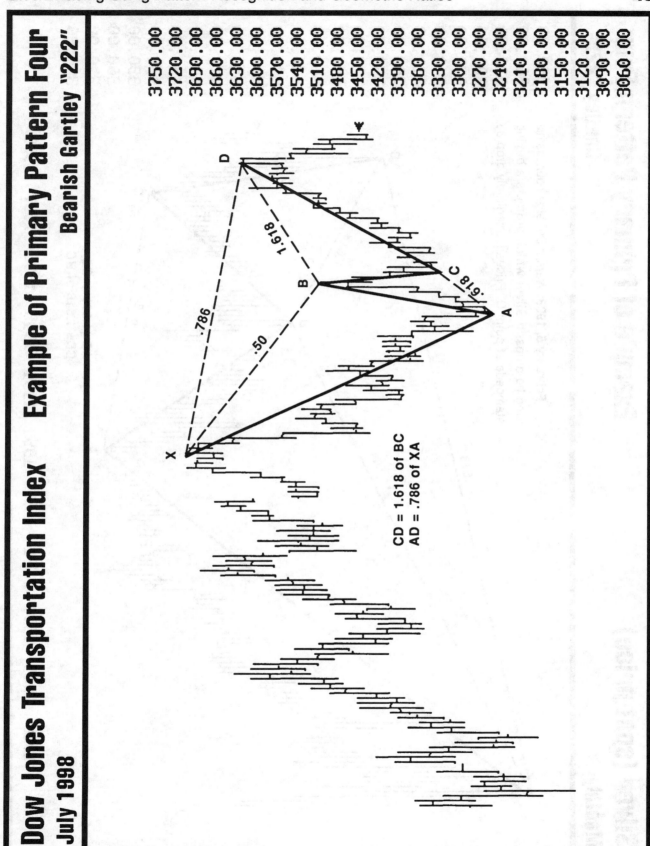

Dow Jones Transportation Index   Example of Primary Pattern Four

July 1998

Bearish Gartley "222"

CD = 1.618 of BC
AD = .786 of XA

.786
.50
1.618
.618

3750.00
3720.00
3690.00
3660.00
3630.00
3600.00
3570.00
3540.00
3510.00
3480.00
3450.00
3420.00
3390.00
3360.00
3330.00
3300.00
3270.00
3240.00
3210.00
3180.00
3150.00
3120.00
3090.00
3060.00

Silver (spot price)
Monthly

Example of Primary Pattern Four
Gartley "222"

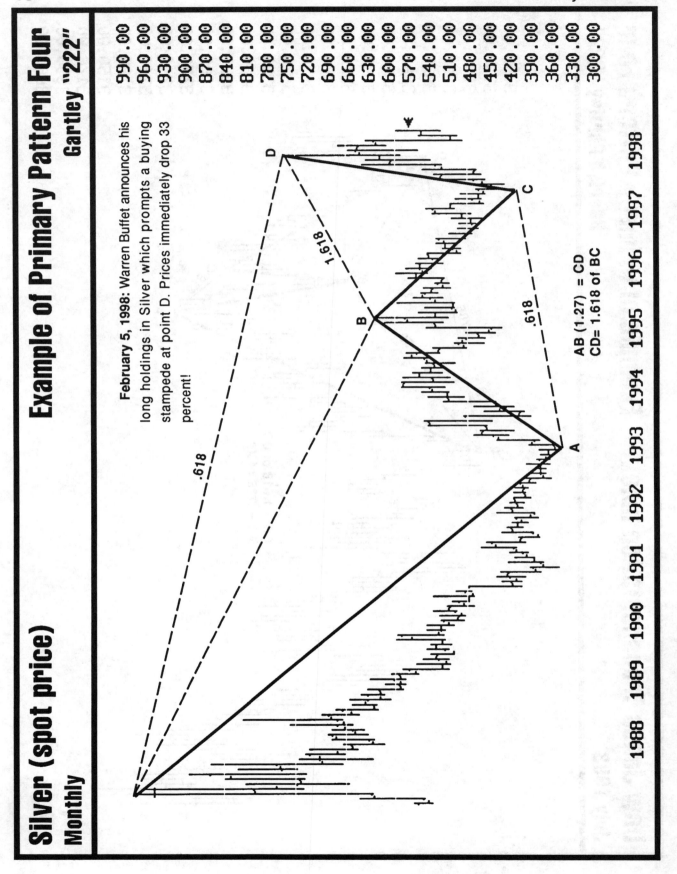

February 5, 1998: Warren Buffet announces his long holdings in Silver which prompts a buying stampede at point D. Prices immediately drop 33 percent!

AB (1.27) = CD
CD= 1.618 of BC

Pattern Five

1. The time frame between point X and point A will be between 5 and 13 time bars (i.e., 5 minute, 30 minute, or daily). On rare instances 21 time bars. These are Fibonacci numbers.

2. There are no swing patterns present between points 1 and A.

3. When the move from X to 1 is very explosive, the pullback to point A may only retrace to 38.2 percent or 50 percent 1X.

4. If the price difference between the .618 and .786 retracement is greater than the trader is willing to risk, the trader should wait for further confirmation (i.e., a change in momentum or candlestick pattern: *doji*, *hammer*). In the S&P 500, for example, if the difference between the .618 and .786 numbers is greater than 1.70 points, I will wait for further confirmation to enter the trade.

5. Time periods, the next swing will usually be dramatic to the downside. If the time frame down from point 1 to A is longer than 8 periods, the ensuing pullback will most likely be less dramatic.

6. The trader will never know which of the retracement numbers the market is going to reach. It is the trader's decision to determine how much risk is in the trade.

7. This pattern forces you to trade with the short term trend. You are not trying to pick a top or bottom.

8. After entry, once prices move 61.8 percent in the direction of the trend, the protective stop should be moved to point A. This gives a risk free trade.

9. The minimum price objective should be the same distance from point A to 1.

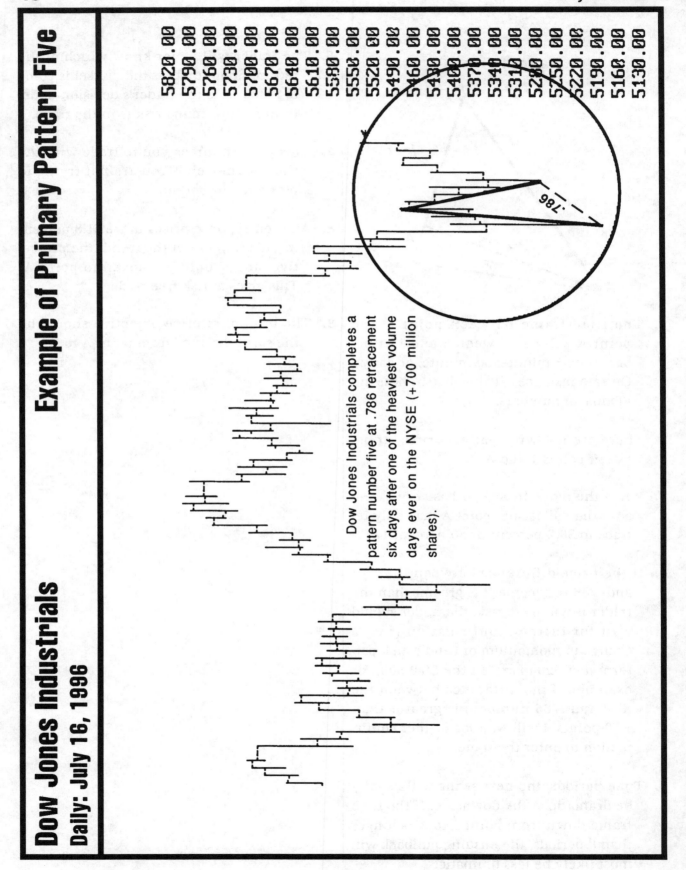

Dow Jones Industrials
Daily: July 16, 1996

Example of Primary Pattern Five

Dow Jones Industrials completes a pattern number five at .786 retracement six days after one of the heaviest volume days ever on the NYSE (+700 million shares).

.786

| 5820.00 |
| 5790.00 |
| 5760.00 |
| 5730.00 |
| 5700.00 |
| 5670.00 |
| 5640.00 |
| 5610.00 |
| 5580.00 |
| 5550.00 |
| 5520.00 |
| 5490.00 |
| 5460.00 |
| 5430.00 |
| 5400.00 |
| 5370.00 |
| 5340.00 |
| 5310.00 |
| 5280.00 |
| 5250.00 |
| 5220.00 |
| 5190.00 |
| 5160.00 |
| 5130.00 |

Anhauser Busch (BUD)
Daily

Example of Primary Pattern Five

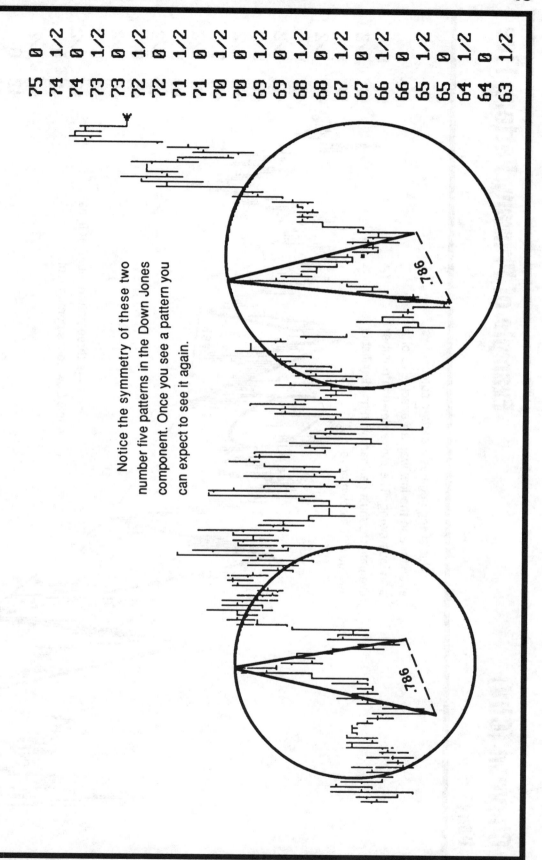

Notice the symmetry of these two number five patterns in the Down Jones component. Once you see a pattern you can expect to see it again.

75	0
74	1/2
74	0
73	1/2
73	0
72	1/2
72	0
71	1/2
71	0
70	1/2
70	0
69	1/2
69	0
68	1/2
68	0
67	1/2
67	0
66	1/2
66	0
65	1/2
65	0
64	1/2
64	0
63	1/2

.786

.786

Chevron (CHV)
Daily

Example of Primary Pattern Five

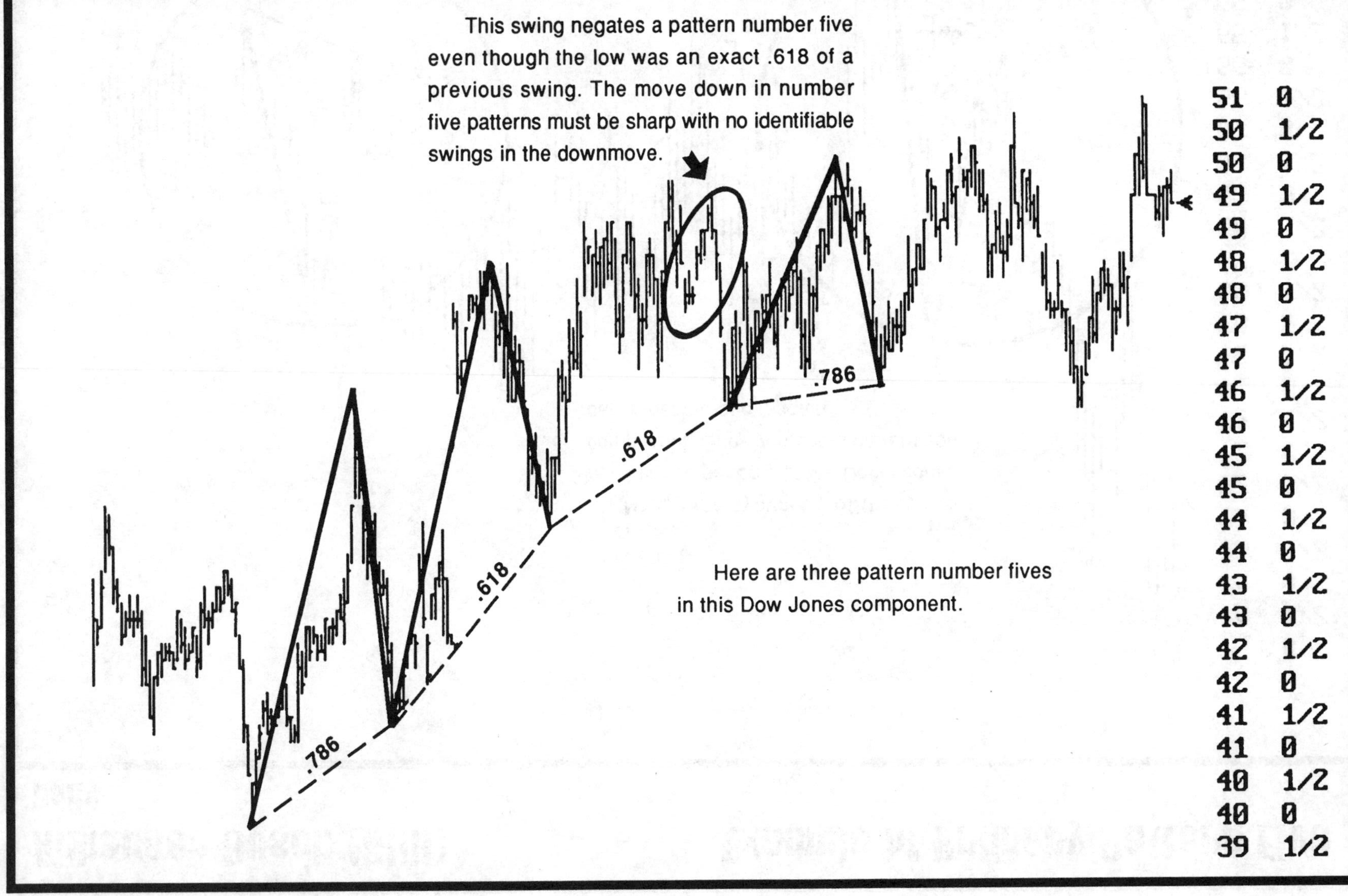

This swing negates a pattern number five even though the low was an exact .618 of a previous swing. The move down in number five patterns must be sharp with no identifiable swings in the downmove.

Here are three pattern number fives in this Dow Jones component.

.786

.618

.618

.786

51	0
50	1/2
50	0
49	1/2
49	0
48	1/2
48	0
47	1/2
47	0
46	1/2
46	0
45	1/2
45	0
44	1/2
44	0
43	1/2
43	0
42	1/2
42	0
41	1/2
41	0
40	1/2
40	0
39	1/2

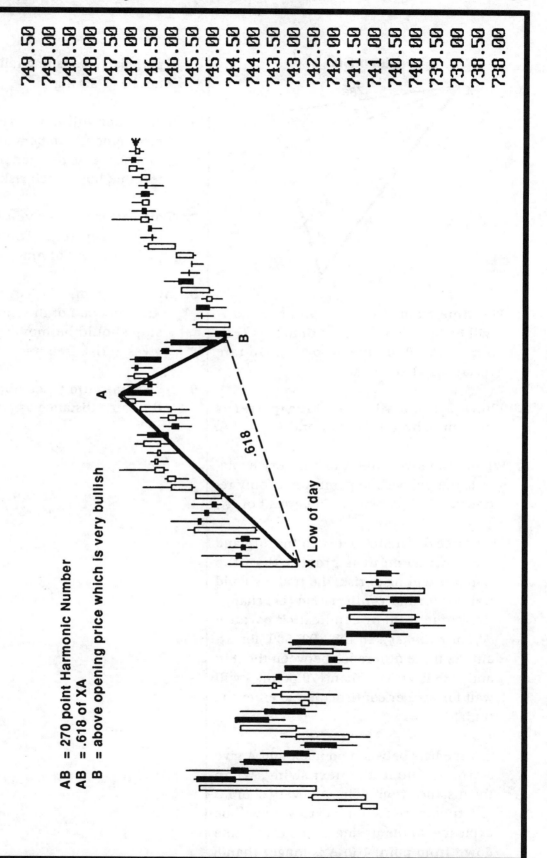

December S&P 500
5 minute

Example of Primary Pattern Five

AB = 270 point Harmonic Number
AB = .618 of XA
B = above opening price which is very bullish

A

B

.618

X Low of day

Pattern Six

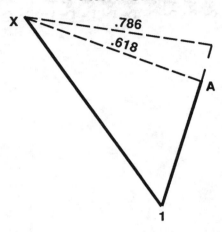

1. The time frame between point X and A will be between 5 and 13 time bars (i.e., 5 minute, 30 minute, or daily). On rare instances 21 time bars.

2. There are usually no swing patterns present between points 1 and A.

3. When the move from X to 1 is very explosive, the pullback to point A may only retrace to 38.2 percent or 50 percent of 1X.

4. If the price difference between the .618 and .786 retracement is greater than the trader is willing to risk, the trader should wait for further confirmation (i.e, change in momentum or candlestick pattern; *doji* or *hammer*). In the S&P 500, for example, if the difference between the .618 and .786 is greater than 170 points I will wait for further confirmation to enter the trade.

5. The time bars between points X and A give a strong clue to the next swing. When the distance from point A is very short, 3 to 5 time periods, the next swing will be explosive to the upside. If the timeframe down from point 1 to A is longer than 8 periods, the ensuing rally will most likely not be as strong.

6. The trader will never know which of the retracement numbers the market is going to reach. It is the trader's decision to determine how much risk is in the trade.

7. This pattern forces you to trade with the short term trend. You are not trying to pick a top or bottom.

8. After entry, once prices move 61.8% in the direction of the trend, the protective stop should be moved to point A. This gives a risk free trade.

9. The minimum price objective should be the same distance as point X to 1.

Example of Primary Pattern Six

December S&P 500
Daily

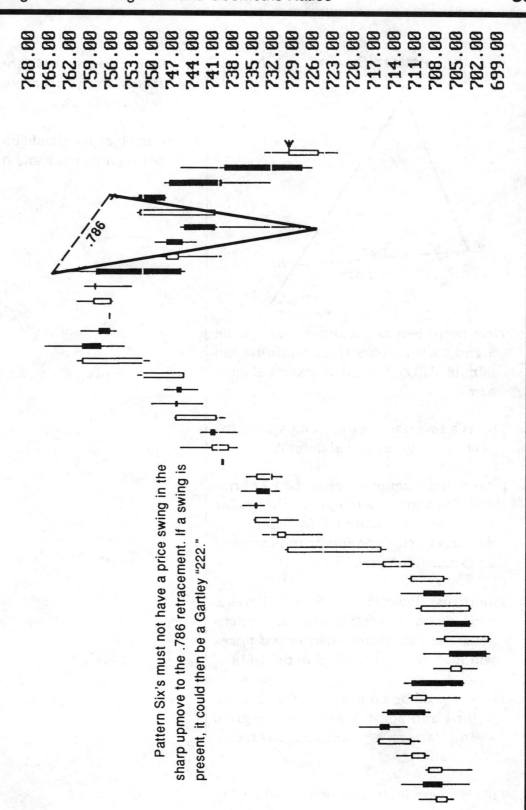

768.00
765.00
762.00
759.00
756.00
753.00
750.00
747.00
744.00
741.00
738.00
735.00
732.00
729.00
726.00
723.00
720.00
717.00
714.00
711.00
708.00
705.00
702.00
699.00

.786

Pattern Six's must not have a price swing in the sharp upmove to the .786 retracement. If a swing is present, it could then be a Gartley "222."

Pattern Seven

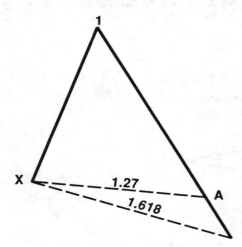

1. Time frame between X and point A will be 5 and 13 time bars (i.e., 5 minute, 30 minute, daily). On rare occasions 21 time bars.

2. This is a reversal or extension pattern. Expect prices to reverse at point A.

3. If the dollar amount between the 1.27 price and 1.618 price is too great, the trader should wait for more confirmation (i.e, *doji* or *hammer* or another indicator) of an exhaustion move.

4. The thrust down from 1 to A will give a good clue as to what to expect. If prices get to the 1.27 within 5 bars or less prices will most probably extend to the 1.618.

5. There should be no price swings between point 1 and point A. If there is a price swing Pattern #6 becomes a Gartley "222" pattern.

6. This is a very important pattern when day trading because point X is often the opening price of the day.

7. When prices react in the direction of the trade, the protective stop should be raised to break even.

8. Profit objective should be the total distance between points 1 and A.

Standard Oil (SO)
Daily

Example of Primary Pattern Seven

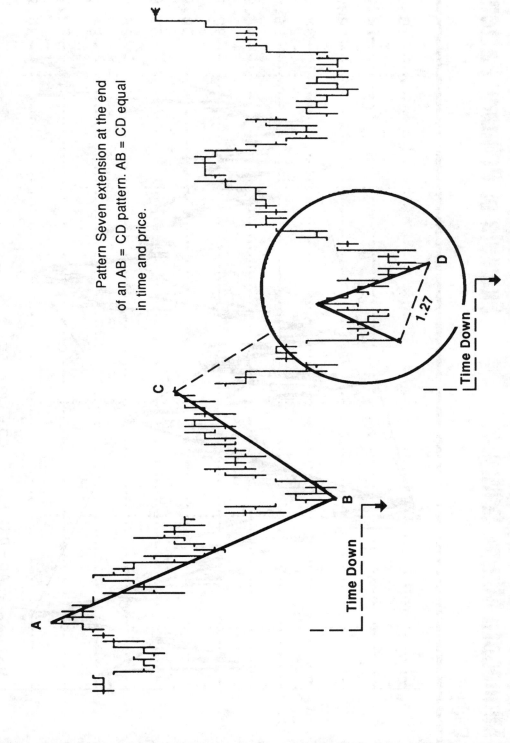

Pattern Seven extension at the end of an AB = CD pattern. AB = CD equal in time and price.

26	1/4
26	0
25	3/4
25	1/2
25	1/4
25	0
24	3/4
24	1/2
24	1/4
24	0
23	3/4
23	1/2
23	1/4
23	0
22	3/4
22	1/2
22	1/4
22	0
21	3/4
21	1/2
21	1/4
21	0
20	3/4
20	1/2

Example of Primary Pattern Eight

Minnesota Mining & Mfg.
Daily

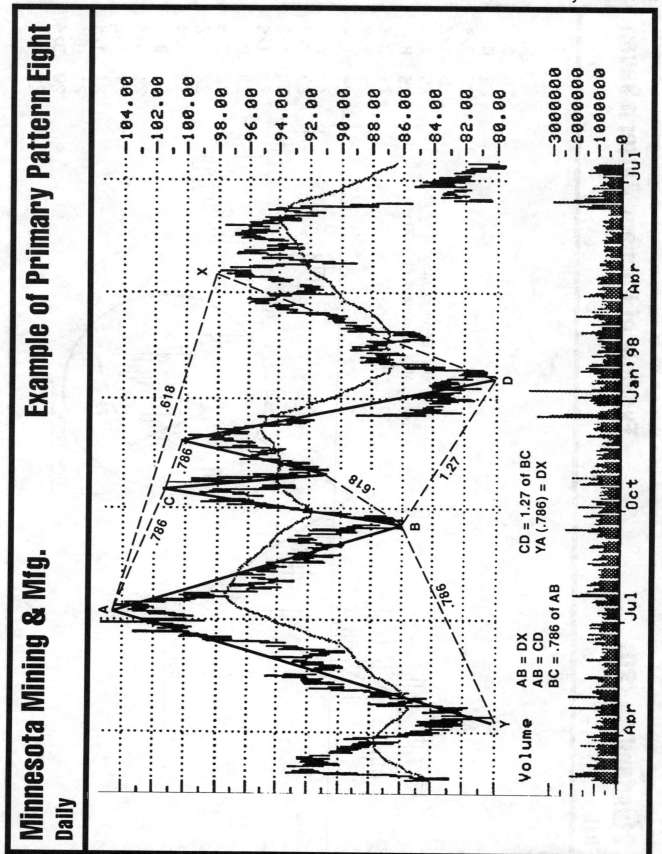

AB = DX
AB = CD
BC = .786 of AB

CD = 1.27 of BC
YA (.786) = DX

Pattern Eight

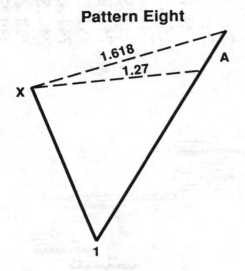

1. Time frame between X and point A will be 5 and 13 time bars (i.e., 5 mminute, 30 minute, daily). On rare occasions 21 time bars.

2. This is a reversal or extension pattern. Expect prices to reverse at point A.

3. If the dollar amount between the 1.27 price and 1.618 price is too great, the trader should wait for more confirmation (i.e., *doji* or *hammer* or another indicator) of an exhaustion move.

4. The thrust down from 1 to A will give a good clue as to what to expect. If prices get to the 1.27 within 5 bars or less prices will most probably extend to the 1.618.

5. There should be no price swings between point 1 and point A. If there is a price swing Pattern #6 becomes a Gartley "222" pattern.

6. This is a very important pattern when day trading because point X is often the opening price of the day.

7. When prices react in the direction of the trade, the protective stop should be raised to break even.

8. Profit objective should be the total distance between points 1 and A.

December S&P 500
5 minute

Example of Primary Pattern Eight

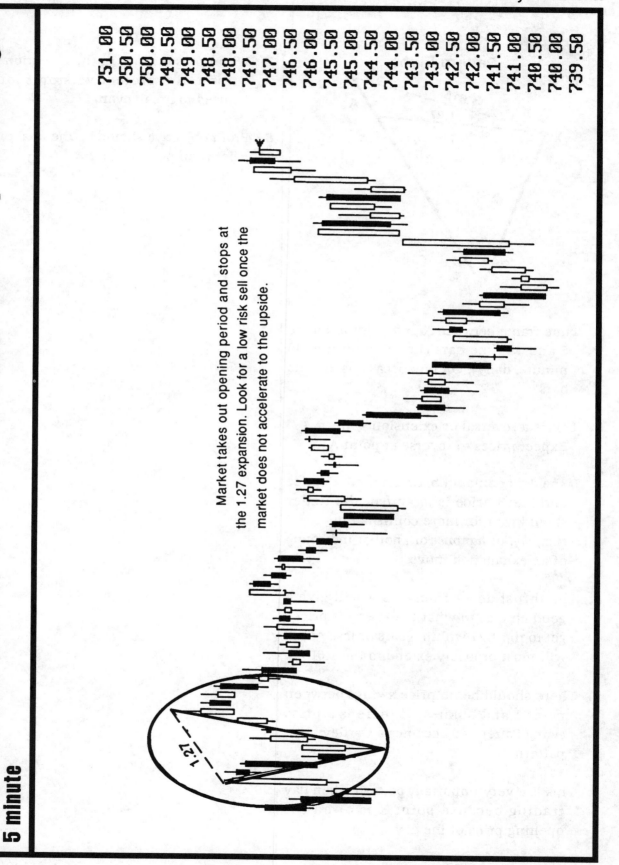

Market takes out opening period and stops at the 1.27 expansion. Look for a low risk sell once the market does not accelerate to the upside.

1.27

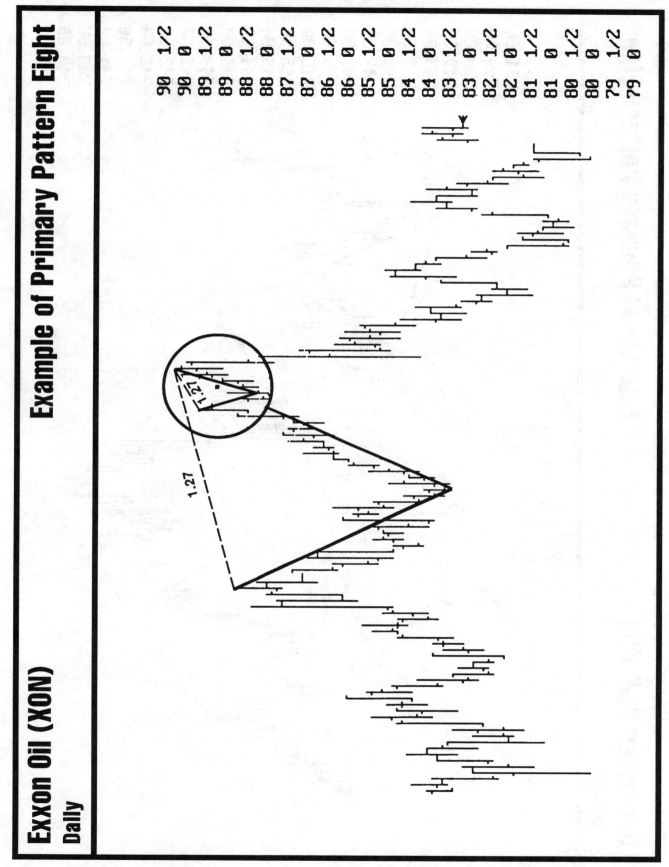

Example of Primary Pattern Eight

Exxon Oil (XON)
Daily

December S&P 500
5 minute

Example of Primary Pattern Eight

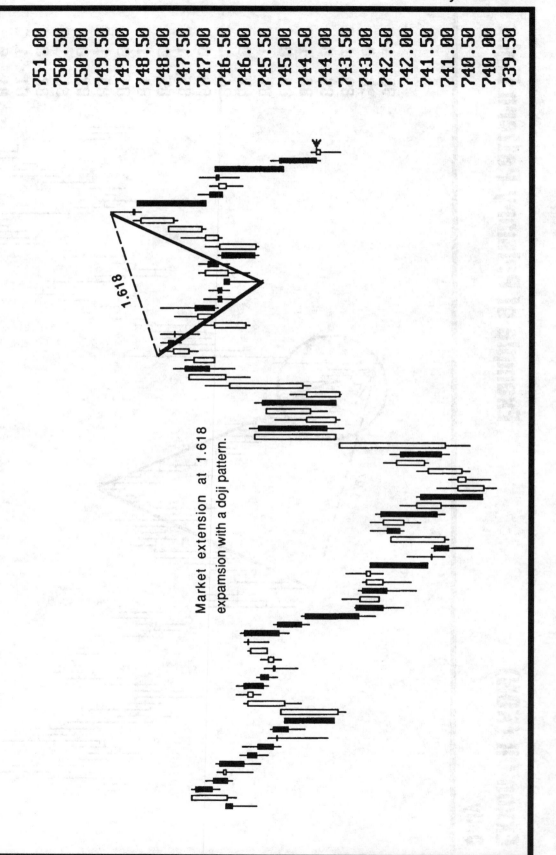

Market extension at 1.618
expamsion with a doji pattern.

1.618

751.00
750.50
750.00
749.50
749.00
748.50
748.00
747.50
747.00
746.50
746.00
745.50
745.00
744.50
744.00
743.50
743.00
742.50
742.00
741.50
741.00
740.50
740.00
739.50

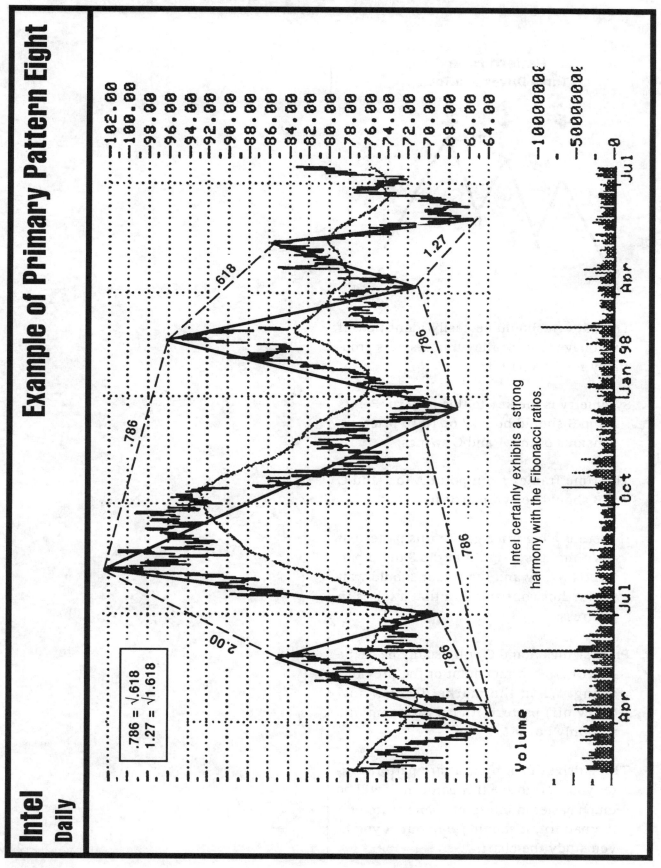

Example of Primary Pattern Eight

Intel
Daily

.786 = √.618
1.27 = √1.618

.618

.786

2.00

1.27

.786

.786

.786

Intel certainly exhibits a strong
harmony with the Fibonacci ratios.

Volume

102.00
100.00
98.00
96.00
94.00
92.00
90.00
88.00
86.00
84.00
82.00
80.00
78.00
76.00
74.00
72.00
70.00
68.00
66.00
64.00

—10000000
—5000000
—0

Apr   Jul   Oct   Jan'98   Apr   Jul

Pattern Nine
Three Drives to a Top

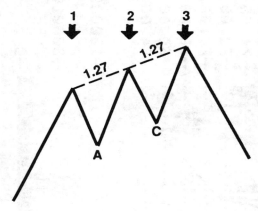

1. The pattern should be easily identified. If you have to force the numbers, it is probably not this pattern.

2. Symmetry is the key to this pattern. Points 2 and 3 should be 1.27 or 1.618 price expansions of the A and C swings.

3. The time frames from point A to 2 and C to 3 should be symmetrical.

4. If there is a big price gap in this pattern at any time it is a sign that the 3 drive pattern is wrong and the trader should wait for further confirmation that a top is in progress.

5. Price swings A and C will usually be at the .618 or .786 retracement of the previous swing. When the market is a vertical (blow off) pattern, these retracements will only be .382.

6. Three drives to a top is a rare pattern. After you start to see this patttern, it will be much easier to interpret. Don't search for the pattern, it should *jump* out at you as you study the chart.

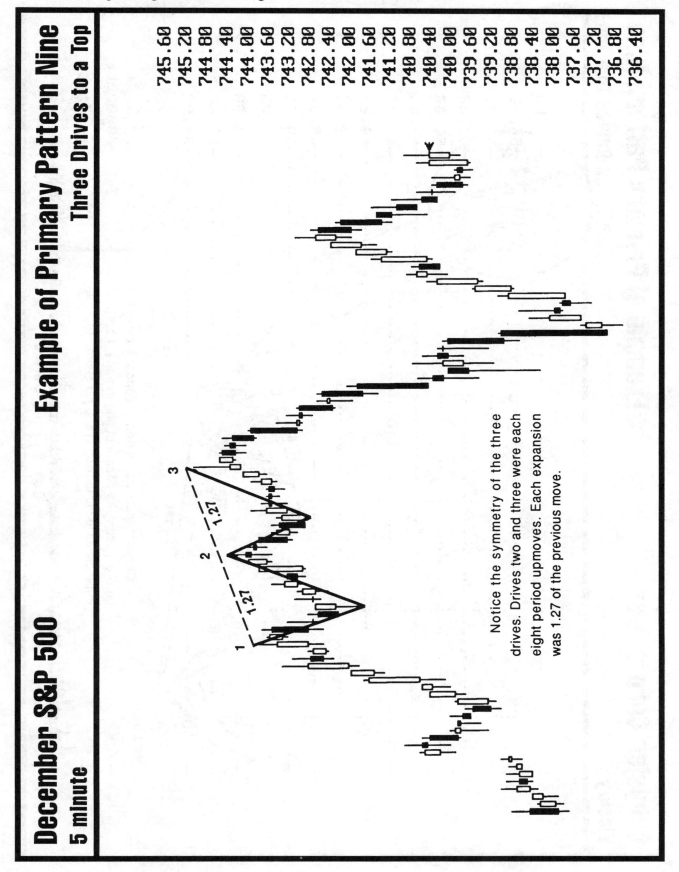

December S&P 500
5 minute

Example of Primary Pattern Nine
Three Drives to a Top

Notice the symmetry of the three drives. Drives two and three were each eight period upmoves. Each expansion was 1.27 of the previous move.

Chrysler Corp.
Weekly

Example of Primary Pattern Nine
Three Drives to a Top

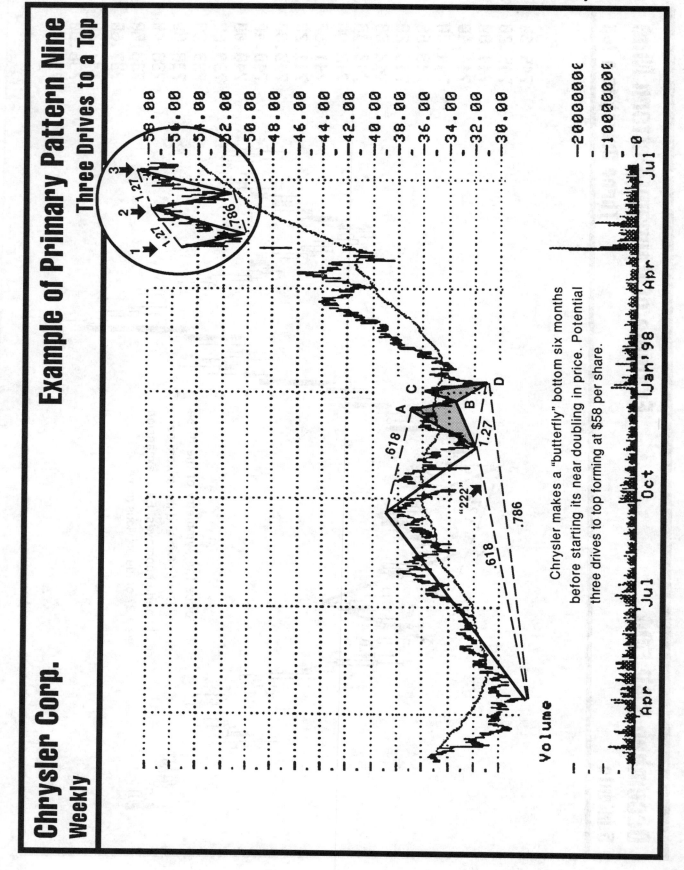

Chrysler makes a "butterfly" bottom six months before starting its near doubling in price. Potential three drives to top forming at $58 per share.

Dow Jones Transportation
Daily

Example of Primary Pattern Nine
Three Drives to a Top

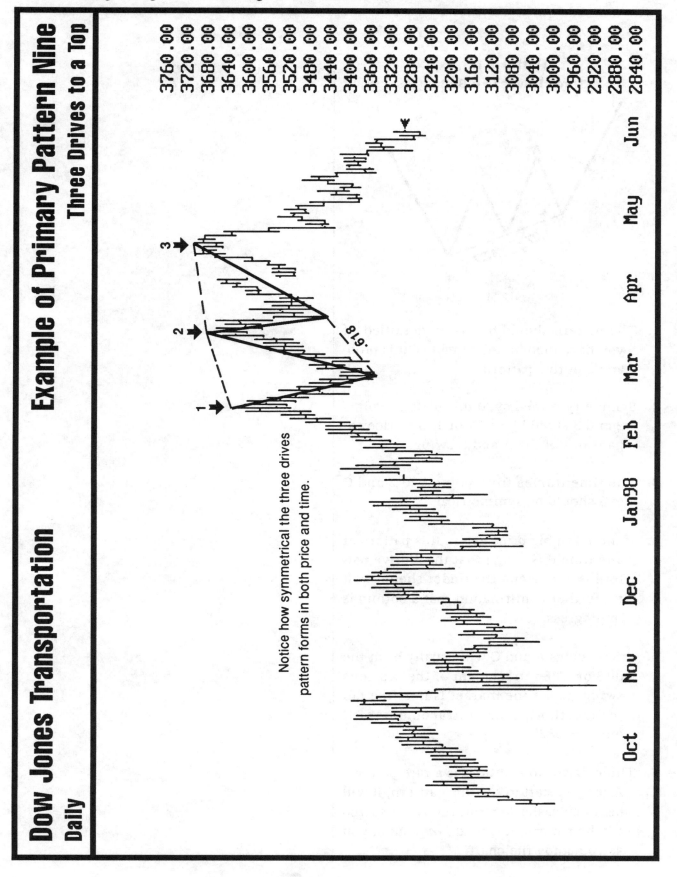

Notice how symmetrical the three drives pattern forms in both price and time.

Pattern Ten
Three Drives to a Bottom

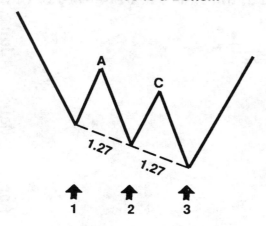

1. The pattern should be easily identified. If you have to force the numbers, it is probably not this pattern.

2. Symmetry is the key to this pattern. Points 2 and 3 should be 1.27 or 1.618 price expansions of the A and C swings.

3. The time frames from point A to 2 and C to 3 should be symmetrical.

4. If there is a big price gap in this pattern at any time it is a sign that the 3 drive pattern is wrong and the trader should wait for further confirmation that a bottom is in progress.

5. Price swings A and C will usually be at the .618 or .786 retracement of the previous swing. When the market is in a free fall (exhaustion), these retracements will only be .382.

6. Three drives to a bottom is a rare pattern. After you start to see this patttern, it will be much easier to interpret. Don't search for the pattern, it should *jump* out at you as you study the chart.

Example of Primary Pattern Ten
Three Drives to a Bottom

December T-Bonds
30 minute

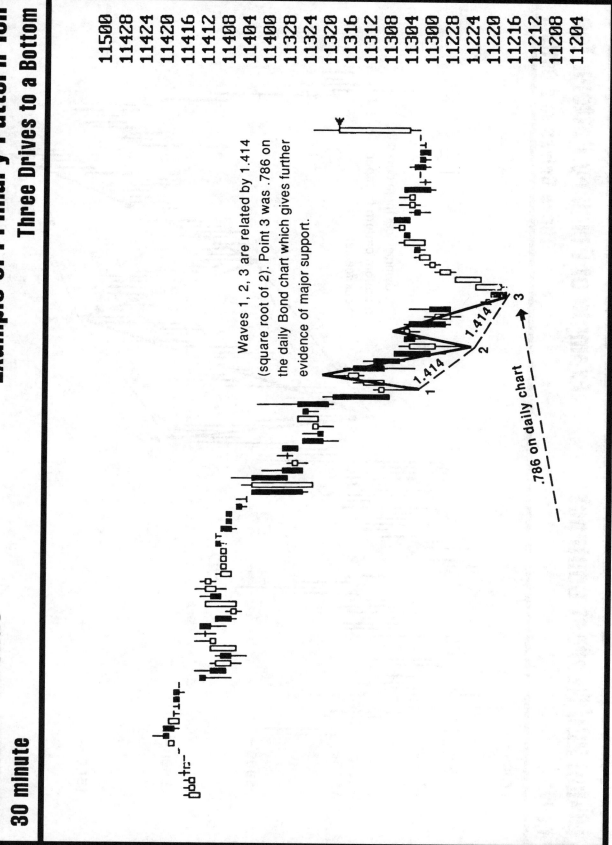

Waves 1, 2, 3 are related by 1.414 (square root of 2). Point 3 was .786 on the daily Bond chart which gives further evidence of major support.

11500
11428
11424
11420
11416
11412
11408
11404
11400
11328
11324
11320
11316
11312
11308
11304
11300
11228
11224
11220
11216
11212
11208
11204

1.414

1.414

1

2

3

.786 on daily chart

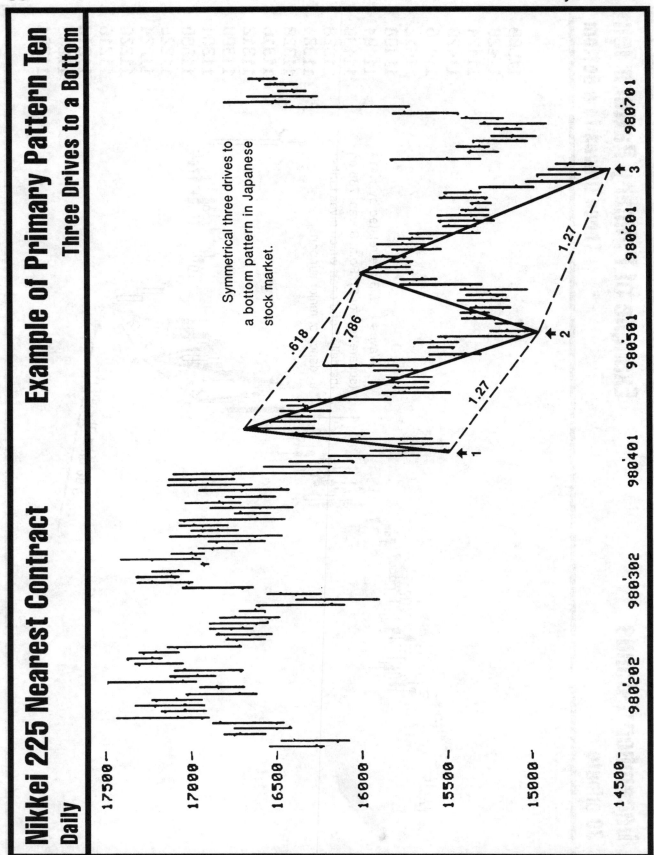

Nikkei 225 Nearest Contract
Daily

Example of Primary Pattern Ten
Three Drives to a Bottom

Symmetrical three drives to a bottom pattern in Japanese stock market.

December S&P
5 minute

Example of Primary Pattern Ten
Three Drives to a Bottom

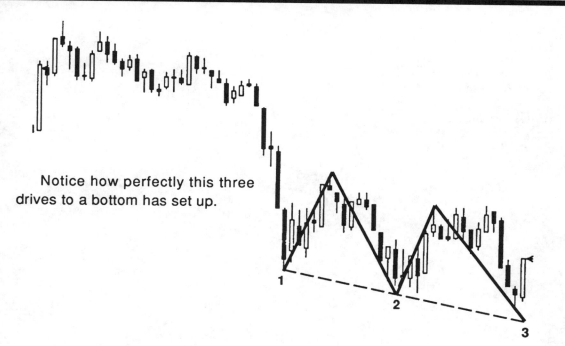

Notice how perfectly this three drives to a bottom has set up.

764.00
763.50
763.00
762.50
762.00
761.50
761.00
760.50
760.00
759.50
759.00
758.50
758.00
757.50
757.00
756.50
756.00
755.50
755.00
754.50
754.00
753.50
753.00
752.50

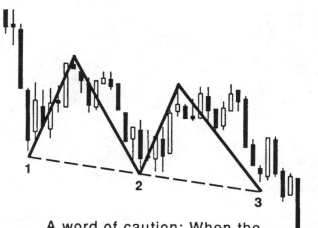

A word of caution: When the three drives pattern fails, it often leads to a huge continuation move in the direction of the trend.

760.00
759.50
759.00
758.50
758.00
757.50
757.00
756.50
756.00
755.50
755.00
754.50
754.00
753.50
753.00
752.50
752.00
751.50
751.00
750.50
750.00
749.50
749.00
748.50

Classical Chart Patterns Using Ratio and Proportion

Those of you who follow the standard trading pattern discussed in technical analysis may find this section interesting. I have selected the four more common patterns traders encounter: Head and Shouders (Bottoms and Tops); Double Bottoms and Tops; Symmetrical Triangles (Broadening Tops and Bottoms); Dynamite Triangles.

If the trader will analyze the pattern using the ratios discussed in this book, it will most probably be enlightening, besides increasing probabilitites of a profitable trade.

December S&P 500
30 minute

Example of Head and Shoulders Pattern

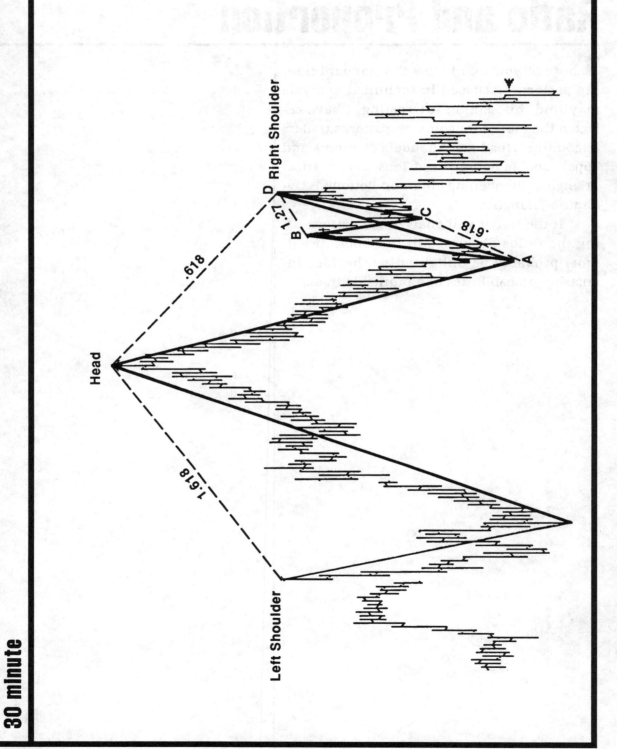

719.25
718.50
717.75
717.00
716.25
715.50
714.75
714.00
713.25
712.50
711.75
711.00
710.25
709.50
708.75
708.00
707.25
706.50
705.75
705.00
704.25
703.50
702.75
702.00

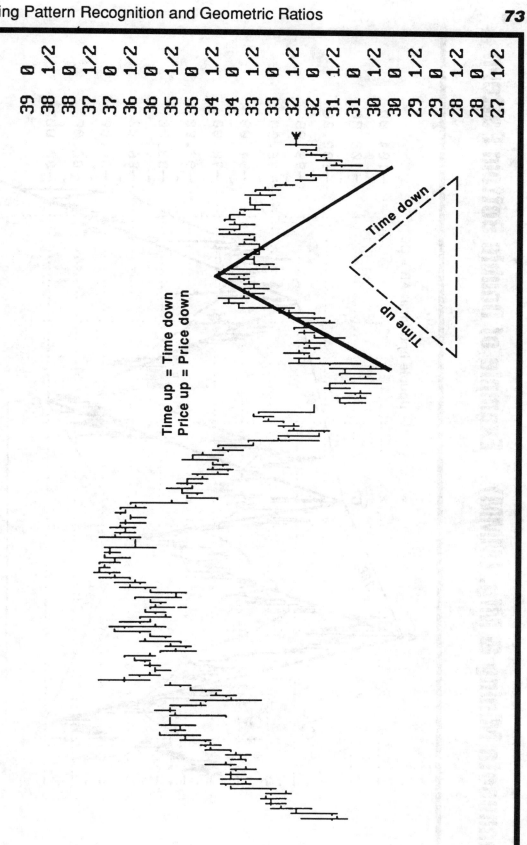

Ford Motors
Daily

Example of Double Bottom Pattern

Minnesota Mining & Mfg. (MMM)   Example of Double Bottom Pattern

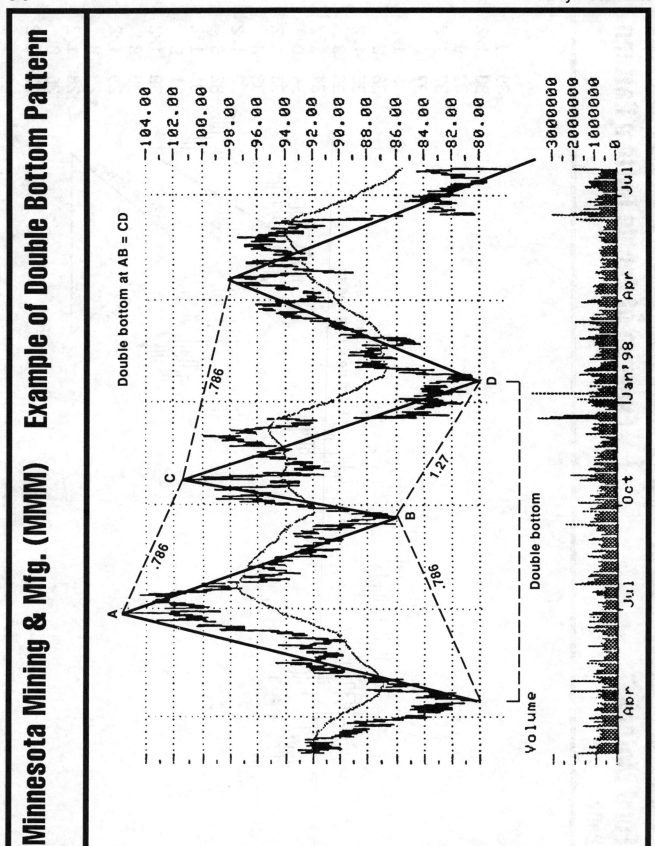

Double bottom at AB = CD

December S&P 500
30 minute

Example of Symmetrical Triangles

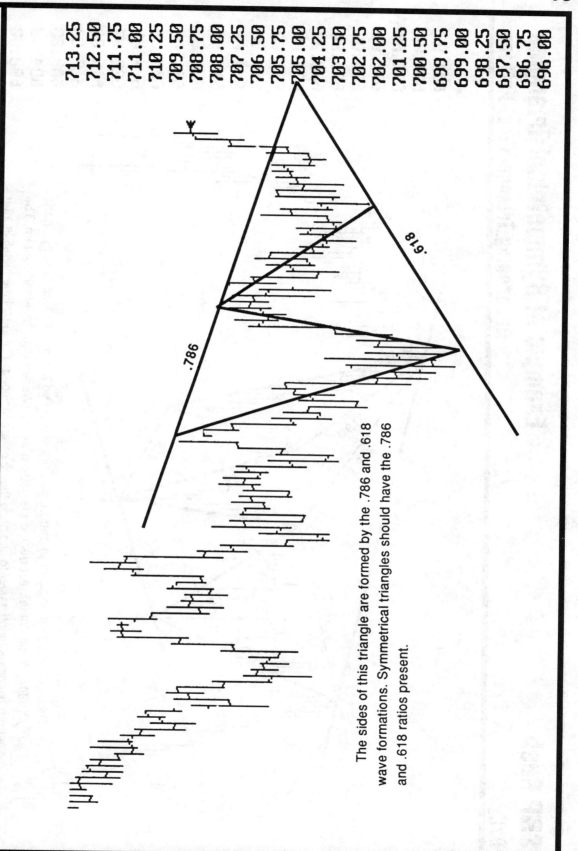

713.25
712.50
711.75
711.00
710.25
709.50
708.75
708.00
707.25
706.50
705.75
705.00
704.25
703.50
702.75
702.00
701.25
700.50
699.75
699.00
698.25
697.50
696.75
696.00

.786

.618

The the sides of this triangle are formed by the .786 and .618 wave formations. Symmetrical triangles should have the .786 and .618 ratios present.

Example of Symmetrical Triangles
Broadening Triangle (Top) Pattern

S&P Cash
Daily

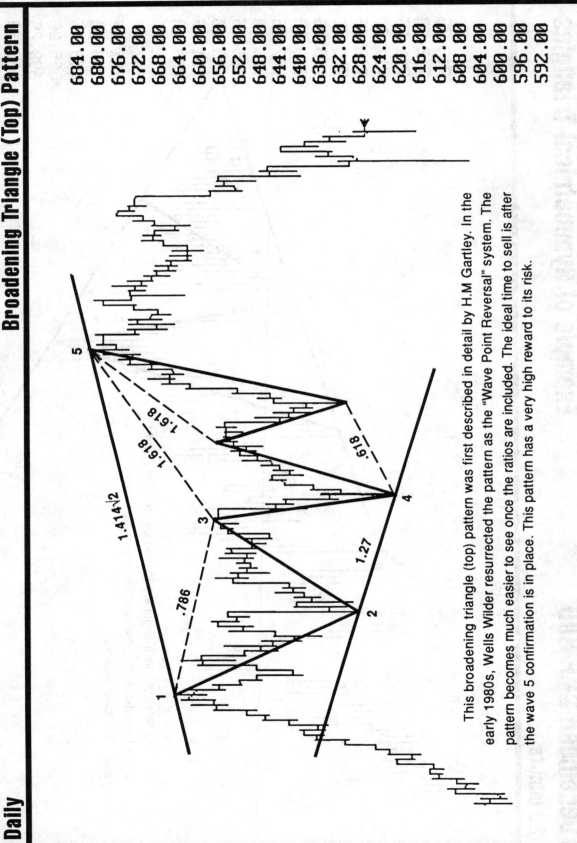

This broadening triangle (top) pattern was first described in detail by H.M Gartley. In the early 1980s, Wells Wilder resurrected the pattern as the "Wave Point Reversal" system. The pattern becomes much easier to see once the ratios are included. The ideal time to sell is after the wave 5 confirmation is in place. This pattern has a very high reward to its risk.

Dow Jones Transportation
Daily

Example of Symmetrical Triangles
Broadening Triangle (Top) Pattern

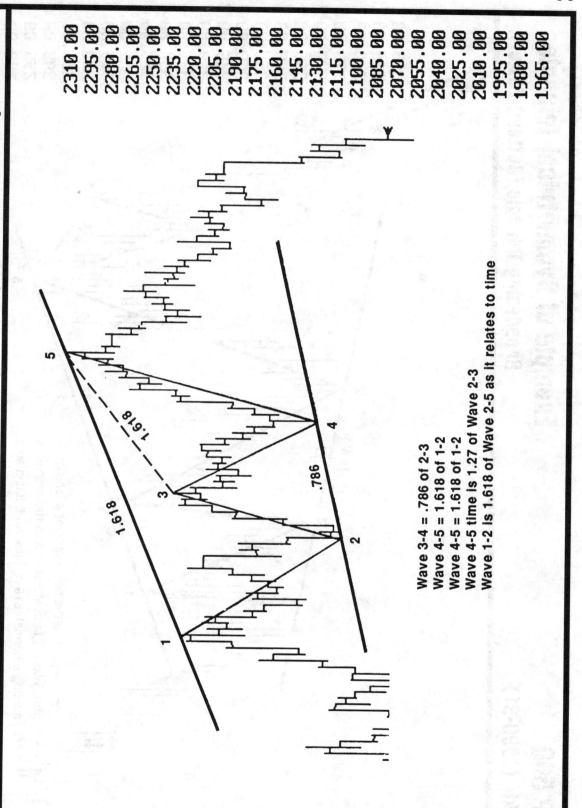

Wave 3-4 = .786 of 2-3
Wave 4-5 = 1.618 of 1-2
Wave 4-5 = 1.618 of 1-2
Wave 4-5 time is 1.27 of Wave 2-3
Wave 1-2 is 1.618 of Wave 2-5 as it relates to time

2310.00
2295.00
2280.00
2265.00
2250.00
2235.00
2220.00
2205.00
2190.00
2175.00
2160.00
2145.00
2130.00
2115.00
2100.00
2085.00
2070.00
2055.00
2040.00
2025.00
2010.00
1995.00
1980.00
1965.00

Example of Symmetrical Triangles
Broadening Triangle (Bottom) Pattern

S&P 500
Weekly (1990-91)

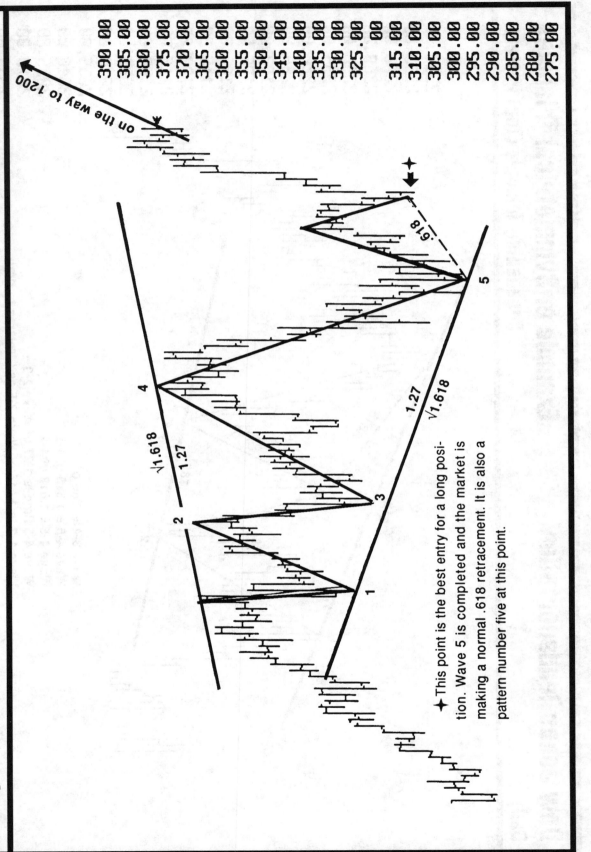

on the way to 1200

390.00
385.00
380.00
375.00
370.00
365.00
360.00
355.00
350.00
345.00
340.00
335.00
330.00
325.00
00
315.00
310.00
305.00
300.00
295.00
290.00
285.00
280.00
275.00

√1.618
1.27

√1.618
1.27

.618

✦ This point is the best entry for a long position. Wave 5 is completed and the market is
making a normal .618 retracement. It is also a
pattern number five at this point.

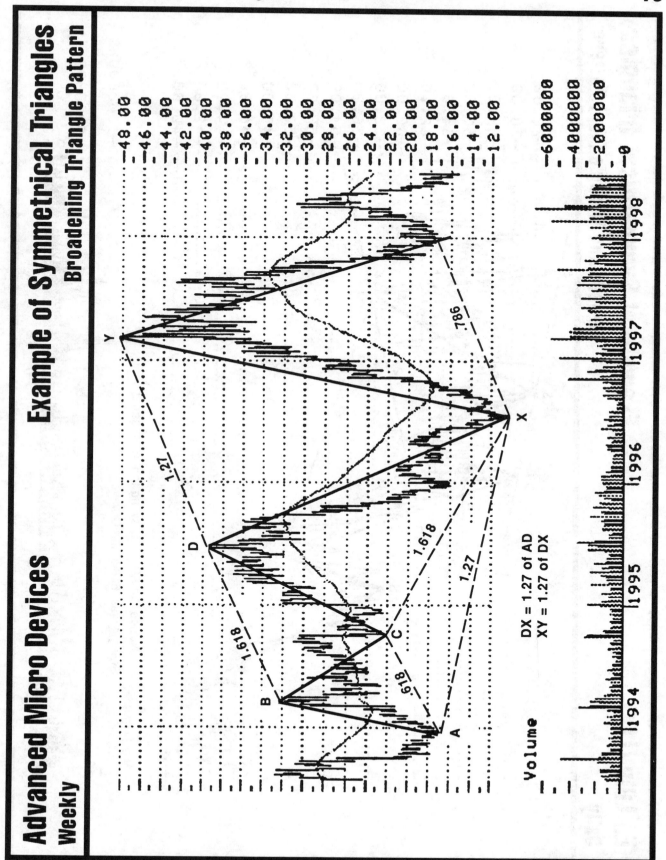

Advanced Micro Devices
Weekly

Example of Symmetrical Triangles
Broadening Triangle Pattern

DX = 1.27 of AD
XY = 1.27 of DX

Volume

Example of Symmetrical Triangles
Broadening Triangle (Top) Pattern

Eli Lilly (LLY)
Daily

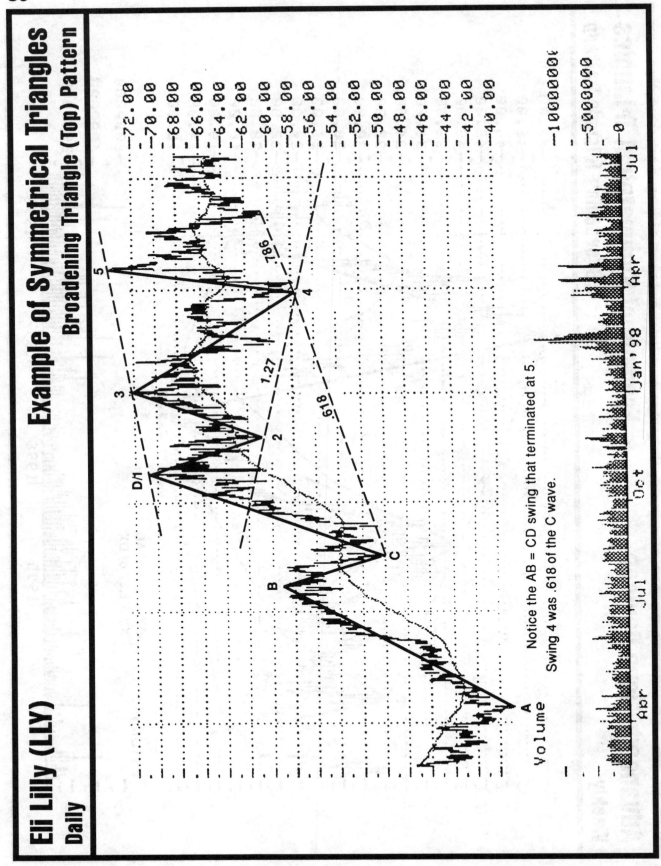

Notice the AB = CD swing that terminated at 5.
Swing 4 was .618 of the C wave.

Microsoft (MSFT)
Daily

Example of Dynamite Triangles
Ascending

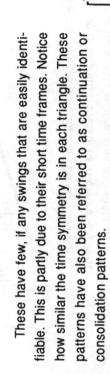

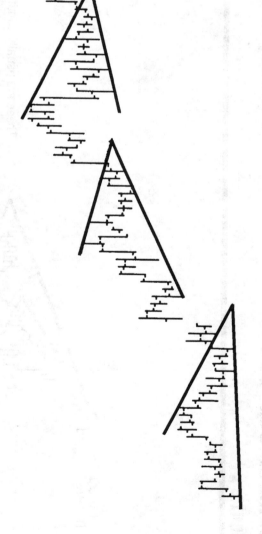

These have few, if any swings that are easily identifiable. This is partly due to their short time frames. Notice how similar the time symmetry is in each triangle. These patterns have also been referred to as continuation or consolidation patterns.

December S&P 500
5 minute

Example of Dynamite Triangles
Descending

These are usually continuation patterns with few, if any swings to calculate. They work immediately or they fail. A pattern of instant gratification or grief. Only minor price swings are located within the triangles.

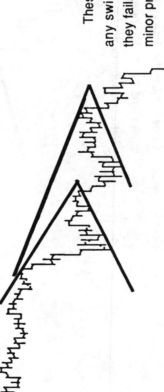

768.00	
766.50	
765.00	
763.50	
762.00	
760.50	
759.00	
757.50	
756.00	
754.50	
753.00	
751.50	
750.00	
748.50	
747.00	
745.50	
744.00	
742.50	
741.00	
739.50	
738.00	
736.50	
735.00	
733.50	

Bonus Pattern: The Butterfly

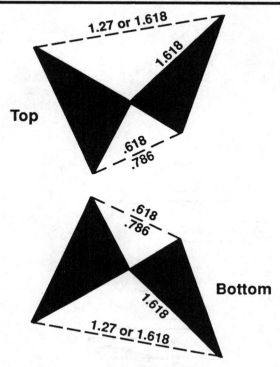

Characteristics of the "Butterfly" Pattern

1. It is formed by the connecting of two triangles.

2. An AB = CD pattern is present in the extension move.

3. The extension move can be either 1.27 or 1.618. Any move beyond 1.618 negates this pattern. Should this occur, a very strong continuation move is in progress.

4. It is found only at significant tops and bottoms.

5. The time bar relationship usually is in ratio and proportion to the price bar.

6. It is correct over 80 percent of the time.

7. The retracement moves inside the butterfly will usually contain .618 and .786 moves.

This pattern was discovered by Bryce Gilmore and myself while we were running analysis routines on his *Wave Trader Software*. It is a very powerful pattern and is seen at significant tops and bottoms only. The "Butterfly' beauty lies in its symmetry. It is my second favorite pattern, just after the Gartley 222.

When several of my close friends reviewed this book for me, they suggested that I omit the Butterfly pattern. I already knew my response to the suggestion. I firmly believe that you can give the trading public the *Holy Grail* and they still don't grasp the principle. The reasons for this are probably related to a general level of skepticism and inability to actually do the work involved. This pattern is far removed from any *Holy Grail*! Find a few on your own and make your own judgement. I know you will find the time well spent.

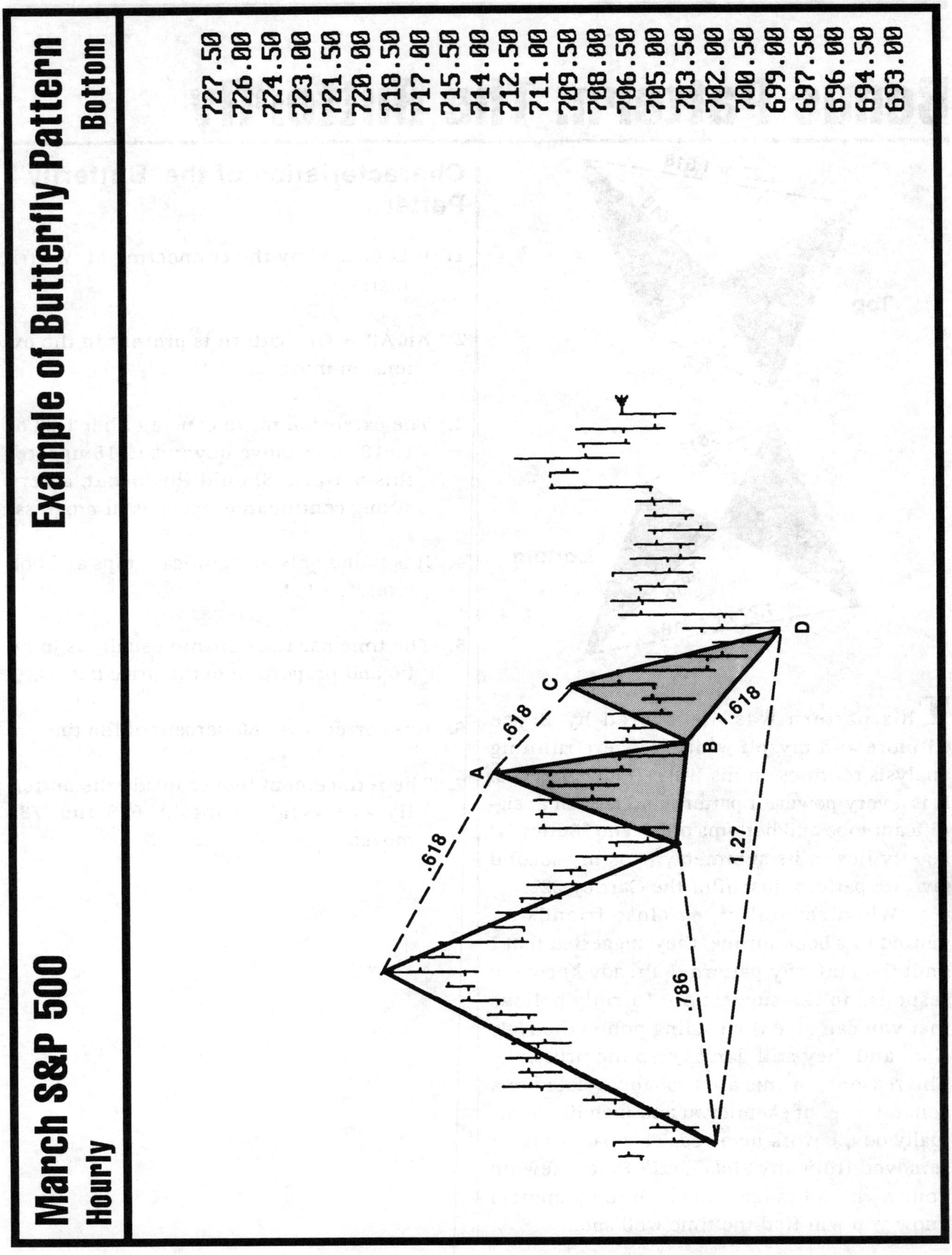

March S&P 500
Hourly

Example of Butterfly Pattern
Bottom

Price
727.50
726.00
724.50
723.00
721.50
720.00
718.50
717.00
715.50
714.00
712.50
711.00
709.50
708.00
706.50
705.00
703.50
702.00
700.50
699.00
697.50
696.00
694.50
693.00

.618

.618

A

.618

C

B 1.618

1.27

.786

D

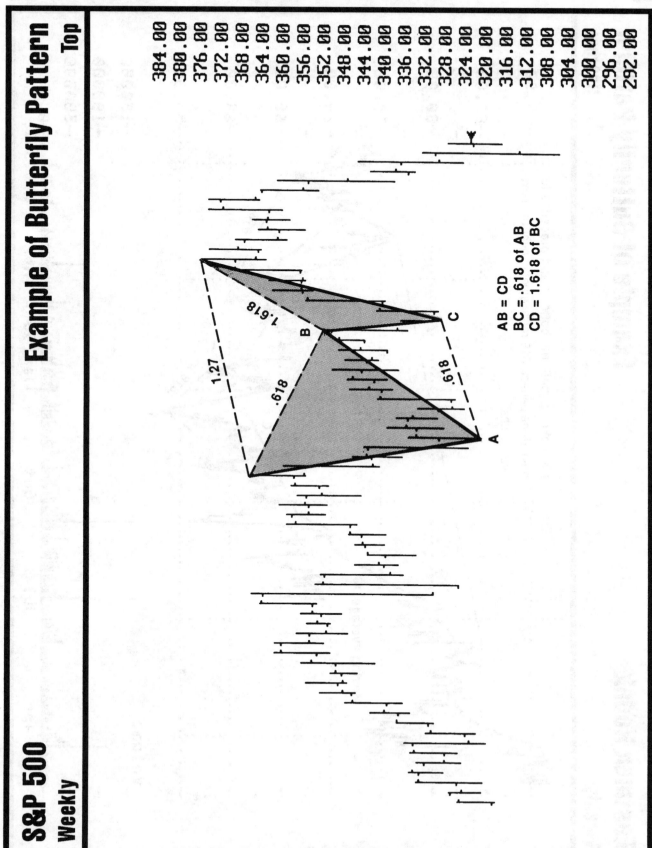

Example of Butterfly Pattern
Top

S&P 500
Weekly

AB = CD
BC = .618 of AB
CD = 1.618 of BC

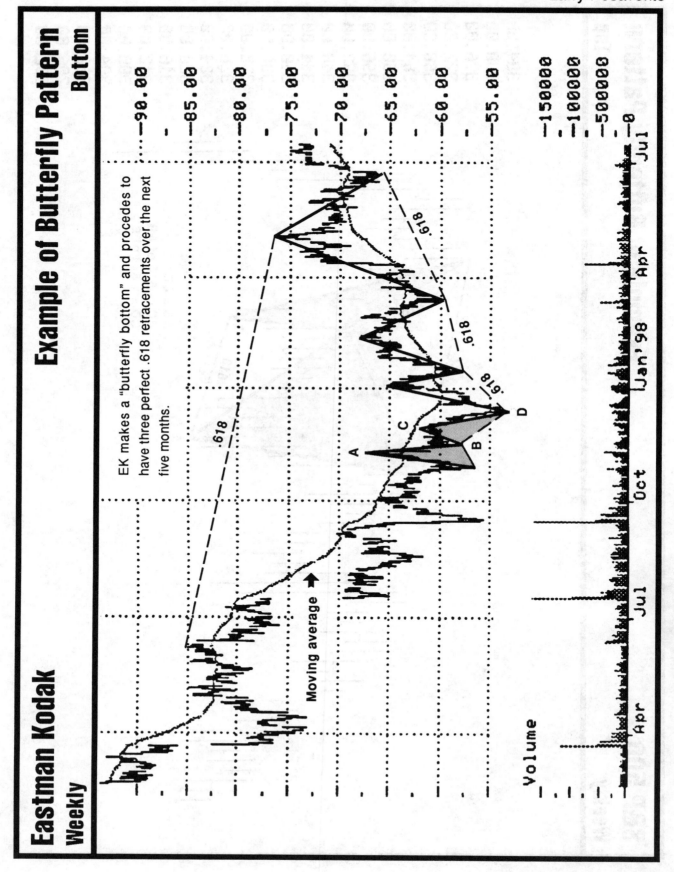

Example of Butterfly Pattern
Bottom

Eastman Kodak
Weekly

EK makes a "butterfly bottom" and procedes to have three perfect .618 retracements over the next five months.

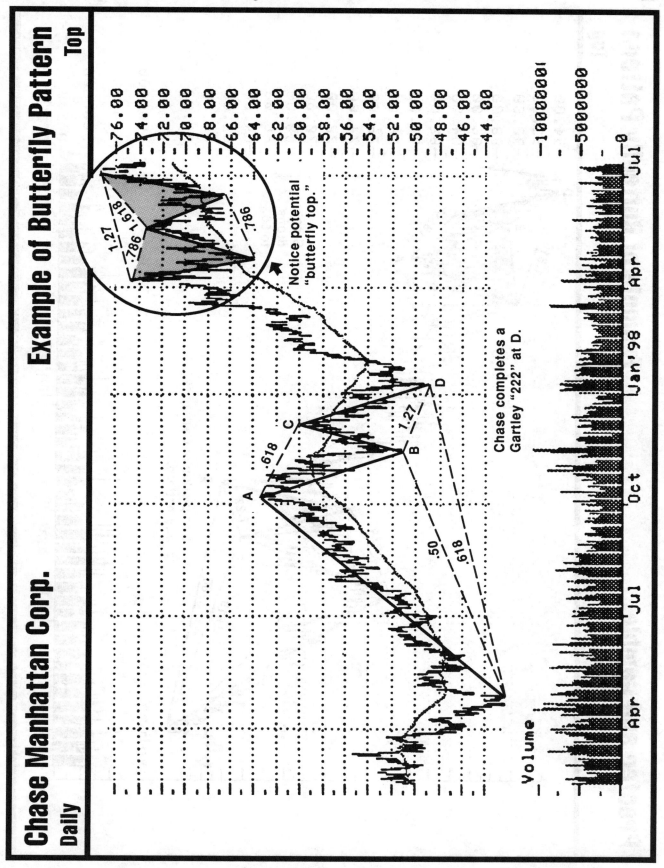

Example of Butterfly Pattern Top

Chase Manhattan Corp.
Daily

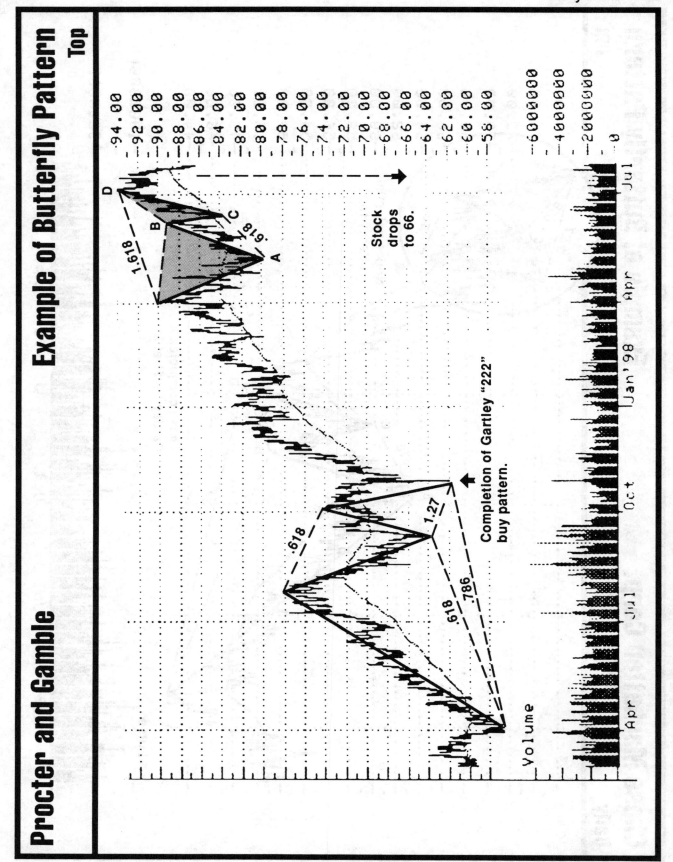

Procter and Gamble

Example of Butterfly Pattern
Top

The Opening Price

I first met John Hill of the Commodity Research Institute in Hendersonville, North Carolina in late 1974 or early 1975. At that time, I was recovering from a tremendous loss in cattle, soybean oil and soybean meal. I was long many contracts during the 1974 October break. I started with nothing, but ran it up to a great deal of money. I then realized that I had the ability to make that kind of money. However, I neglected to realize that I confused success with a bull market and I was unprepared when the bear market finally came.

During these last 23 years, John and I have remained good friends and have shared numerous good trading ideas. In 1982 I went to John's ranch in Hendersonville and spent two weeks with him looking at various ways of trading the markets. One of the best discoveries we made was a computer study which revealed to us the principle called *Trading in the Direction of the Opening Price*. We worked for two solid weeks in several different markets, relating the opening price to the price action of that day. It is probably one of the most amazing statistics that I have ever seen as a technical indicator in trading commodities.

Several years later, Earl Haddady of the Haddady-Sibbett Corporation published the same statistics in a book called *The Importance of the Opening Price*. We heartily recommend this book to anyone interested in trading commodities and especially to those involved in day trading. It puts a tremendous advantage on your side when you're trading in the direction of the opening price.

The principle behind the importance of the opening price probably stems from the fact that the markets are open only six hours a day. That leaves 18 hours for decision making to occur. When you consider the fact that the foreign markets are open in Hong Kong, Tokyo, Singapore, Sidney, London and Amsterdam, you get an even greater flavor of what occurs during the 18 hours when our markets are closed. It is my opinion that decisions are made during the 18 hours that are effected on the opening of our market. I realize that most of the volume is not done on the opening— it is done during the complete day. However, to explain how the opening price is so significant, one must remember that these people have been making thought decisions and analytical decisions during the past 18 hours in order to come up with strategies for the following days.

The Opening Price Principle is this: the opening price will be the high or low of that day 85-90 percent of the time. In other words, the price at the opening will be either within 10 percent of the high or the low of the day on that particular day. There are two ways that you can prove this principle to yourself. First, take a commodity chart like *Commodity Perspective or Futures Charts*, something that shows the opening price which would be the small left-hand bar on the daily bar chart—not the closing price, but the left-hand side which is the opening price. Take a red pencil and draw a little circle around the opening price. Continue that through the life of the contract. Set the chart down and you'll see that the high or the low of the day was the opening price approximately eight or nine times out of 10. The second way to test the importance of the opening price is to use the day trading charts— that is Intraday charts—if you have access to them. Using an intraday chart, mark the opening price and draw a line across the time zone for the rest of the day—a horizontal line where the opening price is indicated. You'll be surprised how often prices meander around that opening price whether it is the high or the low of the day. Even when it's not the high or the low of the day, the opening price seems to be some kind of harmonic or equilibrium price that the market bounces against several times during the day.

Armed with this information, a day trader and, actually, a position trader can enter the market to his advantage with probabilities on his side. The charts on the following pages show examples of how to use the opening price advantage as part of your armamentarium for strategy in entering a market for a position trade and also for profiting on a day trading basis. Keep in mind that this technique does not work all of the time, but that it does put probability in your favor a great deal of the time.

There is an important concept here to remember: forget about the closing price of yesterday. It means absolutely nothing when you're dealing with the opening price concept. Whether the price gaps up or the price gaps down is of no consequence to you when you are using the opening price to enter a market. You must forget the closing price of the previous day; the opening price is your focus, especially when day trading. Whenever I taught this principle, students always seem to want to hang onto the closing price of yesterday. *You must remember not to use yesterday's closing price when using the opening price principle.*

You will see that this technique does get easier with practice as you become more accustomed to its use. The charts on the next several pages present examples of how to use the opening price in conjunction with patterns and pattern recognition formations in order to set up day trading probabilities. You may want to use the "Key of the Day" (Opening + High + Low divided by 3) with this technique. If prices are above Key of Day, only go long. If below Key of Day, only go short.

Keep in mind that in day trading—and also position trading—you must be concerned with both the Price and the Time Axis. Some people who day trade will inadvertently lose money because they forget about the Time Axis. They think they are trading just for several days when, in fact, they put a trade on for a day trade and it turns into a position trade which gaps the opposite of what position they are holding, resulting in a loss. When you are day trading, you should be out on the close. If you are position trading, you should position yourself for a longer term move somewhere in the neighborhood of three days to three months, depending on your style of trading.

One of our favorite day trading techniques is to buy that (.618) retracement from the opening price with a stop at the (.85) retracement. In other words, if the market dropped more than 25 percent below the (.618) you would be able to say that you were wrong; your stop limitation is very small and you would be able to profit as the market moved higher. The Microsoft chart on page 92 illustrates this point perfectly. The market did, in fact, move higher and you turned a profit at the end of the day.

Two important things to remember when day trading: 1) Get a very fair commission rate. A $25 - $30 range is completely acceptable. 2) Good volatility is essential. Trade the markets that are quite volatile and highly active with a great deal of volume.

Examine the following intraday charts (Yahoo, Intel, Pfizer and September S&P 500) and you will see how the opening price fits nicely with intraday Fibonacci retracements.

Remember: Trade in the direction of the opening price. If athe prices are **below** the opening price, look for (.618) or (.786) intraday rally to get short. If prices are **above** the opening price, look for a (.618) or (.786) to get long.

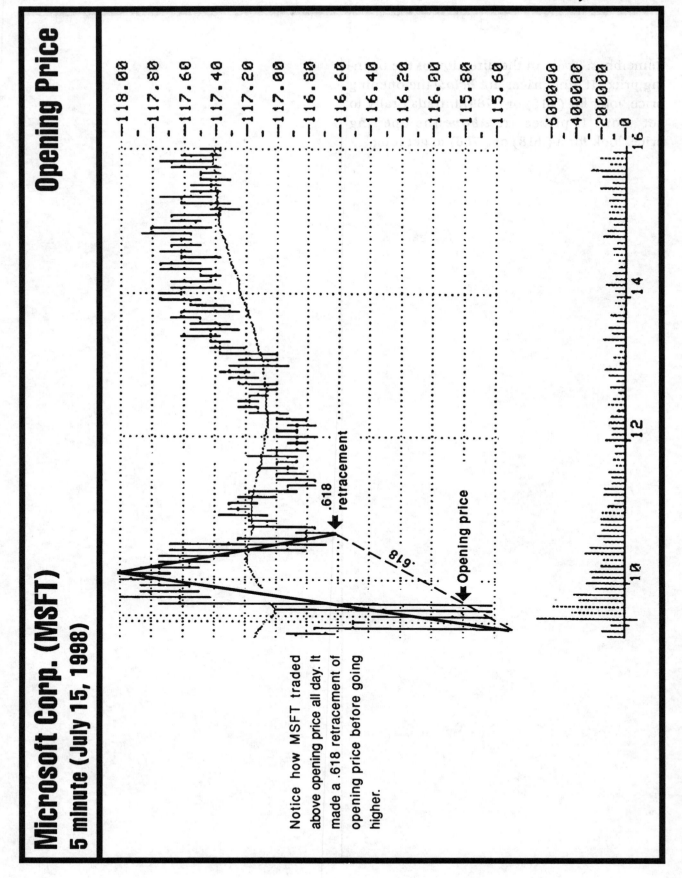

Microsoft Corp. (MSFT)
5 minute (July 15, 1998)

Opening Price

.618 retracement

.618

Opening price

Notice how MSFT traded above opening price all day. It made a .618 retracement of opening price before going higher.

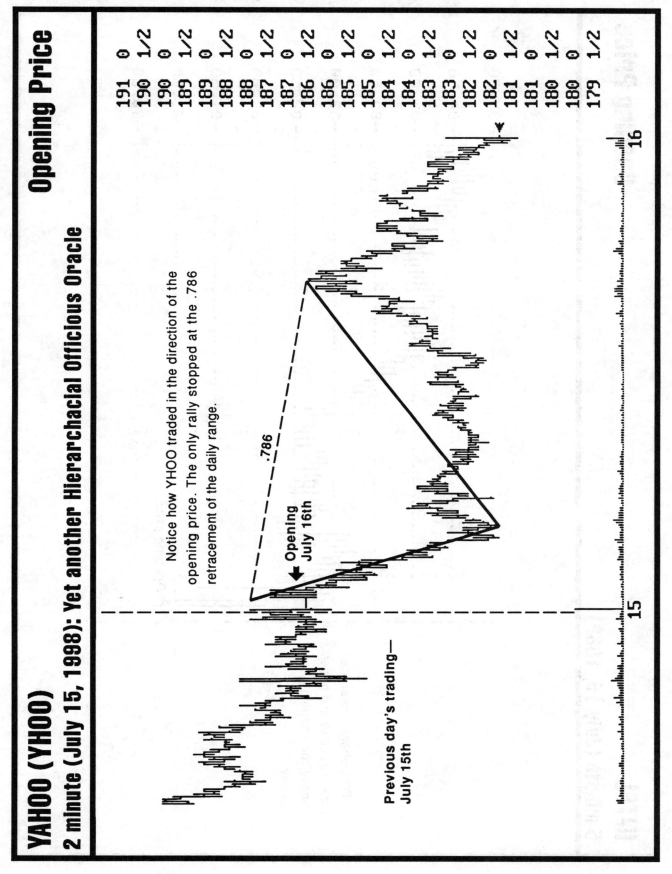

YAHOO (YHOO)
2 minute (July 15, 1998): Yet another Hierarchacial Officious Oracle

Opening Price

Notice how YHOO traded in the direction of the opening price. The only rally stopped at the .786 retracement of the daily range.

.786

Opening
July 16th

Previous day's trading—
July 15th

Opening Price

INTEL
5 minute (July 15, 1998)

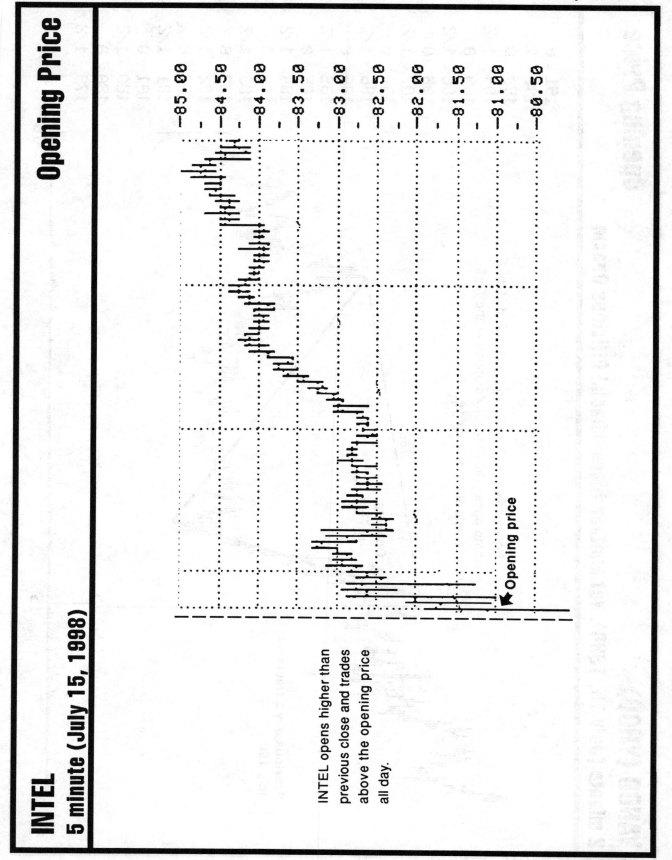

INTEL opens higher than previous close and trades above the opening price all day.

Opening price

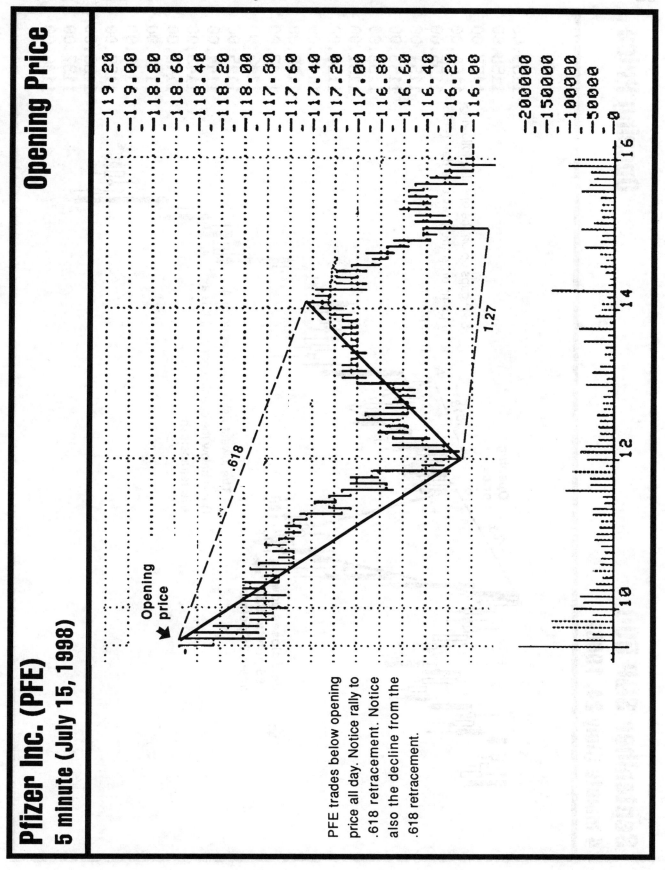

Pfizer Inc. (PFE)
5 minute (July 15, 1998)

Opening Price

PFE trades below opening price all day. Notice rally to .618 retracement. Notice also the decline from the .618 retracement.

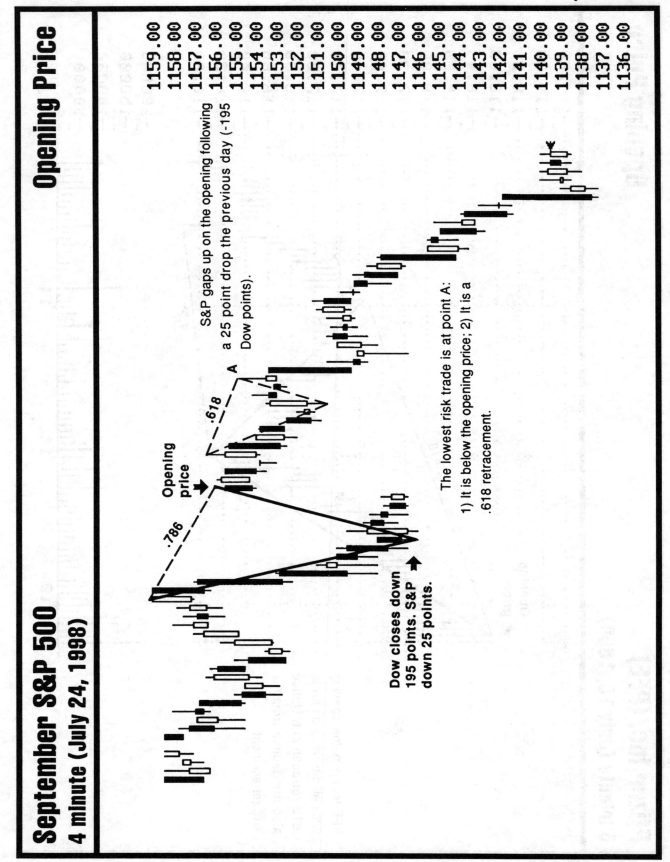

September S&P 500
4 minute (July 24, 1998)

Opening Price

S&P gaps up on the opening following
a 25 point drop the previous day (-195
Dow points).

The lowest risk trade is at point A:
1) It is below the opening price; 2) It is a
.618 retracement.

Dow closes down
195 points. S&P
down 25 points.

Opening
price

.786

.618

A

1159.00
1158.00
1157.00
1156.00
1155.00
1154.00
1153.00
1152.00
1151.00
1150.00
1149.00
1148.00
1147.00
1146.00
1145.00
1144.00
1143.00
1142.00
1141.00
1140.00
1139.00
1138.00
1137.00
1136.00

Entry Techniques

Here are some of my favorite entry techniques used in conjunction with the geometric patterns. They are listed in their order of importance (importance to me!)

The Shapiro Iteration

Described in the following pages.

Limit Orders

Placed a few ticks above or below the exact geometric price measurements. A predetermined stop loss (approxiamtely $600) is placed at the same time.

Candlestick Patterns

These patterns graphically display the importance of the trading range for that time emphazing the opening price. Here are four favorite patterns:

Tweezers—This formation is the equivalent of a double bottom. Tweezers occur when 2 lines have equal highs or lows in succession. They help to quantify risk at the completion of the geometric patterns.

Dojis—The market opened and closed at the same price after making the highs and lows. They occur when the market is in transition from bullish to bearish mode or vice versa. Doji's are even more important at the end of a geometric pattern. This is also true when they occur after very volatile markets. It is a sign that *all* of the market players—bulls and bears—are nervous.

Hammers—The hammer is a period when the market has met strong support after a sharp sell off. It gets its name from "hammering out a bottom." A hammer should be twice the length of the candle. Hammer should be esthetically easy to see. If you have a doubt, it is probably not a hammer.

Shooting Stars—These are accompanied by an upside gap on the opening with the market closing near the lower end of the trading range. These are particularly useful entry techniques at the end of the geomtetric pattern. They appear as the opposite of the hanging man.

Many other candlestick patterns may be helpful as well. I only use these four because they seem to go hand-in-hand with the geometric patterns.

The Shapiro Iteration

When I day trade and use only one calculation to decide on an entry or exit value, I apply what I like to call the "Shapiro Iteration" before putting on the trade. It involves waiting one bar value of whatever the time value is of the chart I am using to decide on the trade. For example, I wait five minutes if I am using a five minute chart to make trading decisions, 30 minutes if I am using a 30 minute chart, etc. It was proposed by Steve Shapiro one day after the market went against him, literally almost before he had put the phone back into its cradle after placing an order. Like the rest of us, he too, has made decisions using emotion rather than logic more times than he cares to admit. Since we bagan applying it, the technique has saved both of us a great deal of money. There is more than one lesson in his explanation of what he calls his "Five Minute Rule," but what I call the "Shapiro Iteration."

The most difficult thing for any trader to do is isolate the emotional part of his thinking and keep it from interfering with his trading. One of the best ways to accomplish this task is to plan and place both the entry point and price objective before you make the trade.

Including both of these price points with a stop loss when you place your original order will reduce the emotional element of trading. The problem with this concept is that, for whatever reason, most traders simply cannot operate this mechanically.

It is necessary, therefore, to be realistic and try to develop a safety valve that can protect us from ourselves if we cannot behave this rationally. The closest concept to a fail-safe rule I have found to use in the heat of trading is the "Shapiro Iteration" or "Five Minute Rule."

When a decision to put on a trade is made during market hours, it is often made on the basis of only one calculation, rather than the more reliable confirmation of a number of decisions drawing the same or similar conclusions about price.

Many times as we sit and watch the screen we experience the urge to make a trade because it is beginning to move in the direction we anticipated. We saw the trade before the move began, but for some reason did not put it on.

As the price moves our way, and particularly if it begins to accelerate, there is an emotional surge we experience that comes from a combination of being right about the trade, and feeling indecisive about not putting it on, as well as guilty/angry about losing the profit. It is precisely this eagerness to still want to "hop on the train before it gets too far from the station" that usually gets us in trouble. Unless the price action suddenly slows down drastically, or reverses altogether, the emotional surge will continue to swell and many times we will put on the trade, even though we logically know it is not the best course of action.

The result is too often what appears to be the vengeance of the trading gods. We have all had the experience of struggling with ourselves about placing such an order, and when we finally make the decision to do it, almost as soon as we put the phone back in the cradle the price action changes. We almost believe that the market was active and alive and just waiting for the exact moment we put on our one or two contracts to reverse the price movement.

It is especially important at these times to remember that when this happens, the market is not alive or right or wrong, and it is not punishing us for doing the wrong thing. The market simply and always just is. It is we who are right or wrong. It is we who punish ourselves for anger, or greed or indecision or not doing our homework.

After acting more times than I care to admit on this emotional impulse to place the right trade at the wrong time, a very simple conclusion presented itself. Because the time between actually putting on the trade and the time the market seemed to reverse was so small, (often it seemed to happen simultaneously no matter how hard I tried to "outsmart" or "beat" the market), the only logical way to deal with this seemingly insurmountable temptation was to write down the exact time and price when I finally decided to make the trade, and force myself to wait at least five minutes, 300 seconds, before actually initiating it.

The logic was elegant in its simplicity. If the trading gods really were waiting in ambush for my emotions to drive me to make the trade at exactly the wrong moment, in five minutes I would observe a noticeable change in trend in the price action, proof that I should not have put on the trade.

When this is the case, the amount saved usually turns out to be substantial. This is true for two reasons. First, when the price reverses after a fast move in one direction, it is often an equally speedy and sizable retracement of the previous move. If I placed a close stop to limit the loss, it is usually hit rather quickly. If a stop was not put on, it became a destructive game of playing catch up and possibly letting a small loss that should not have occurred in the first place develop into a larger loss. When this happens your focus usually follows the loss instead of looking for another profitable situation.

If, in fact, the trade still looked good five minutes after my emotions told me I couldn't wait a minute longer, then all I did was lose a little of the profit that was still to be made. In either case the net is still a gain.

December S&P 500
5 minute

Example of Entry Technique
The Shapiro Iteration

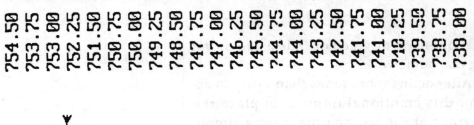

754.50
753.75
753.00
752.25
751.50
750.75
750.00
749.25
748.50
747.75
747.00
746.25
745.50
744.75
744.00
743.25
742.50
741.75
741.00
740.25
739.50
738.75
738.00
737.25

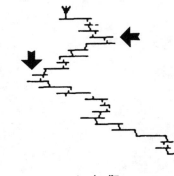

Arrows illustrate the principle behind The Shapiro Iteration. Wait for the market to confirm support or resistance by having one or more inside trading bars near the completing of the geometric patterns.

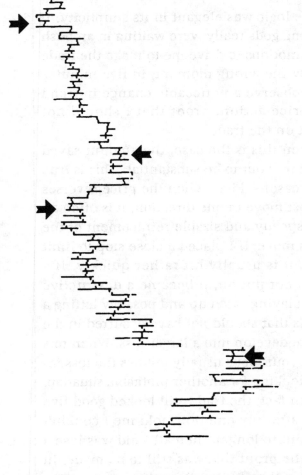

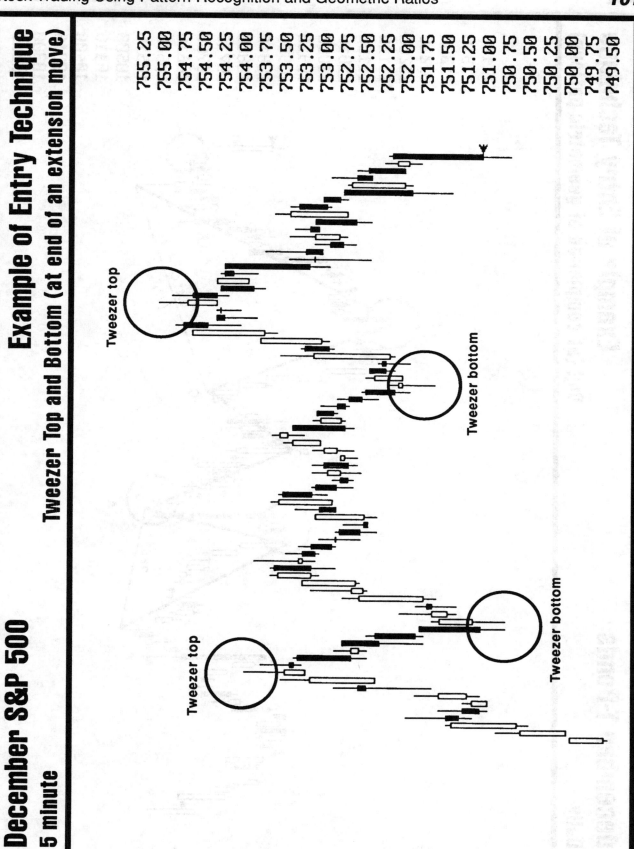

December S&P 500
5 minute

Example of Entry Technique

Tweezer Top and Bottom (at end of an extension move)

Larry Pesavento

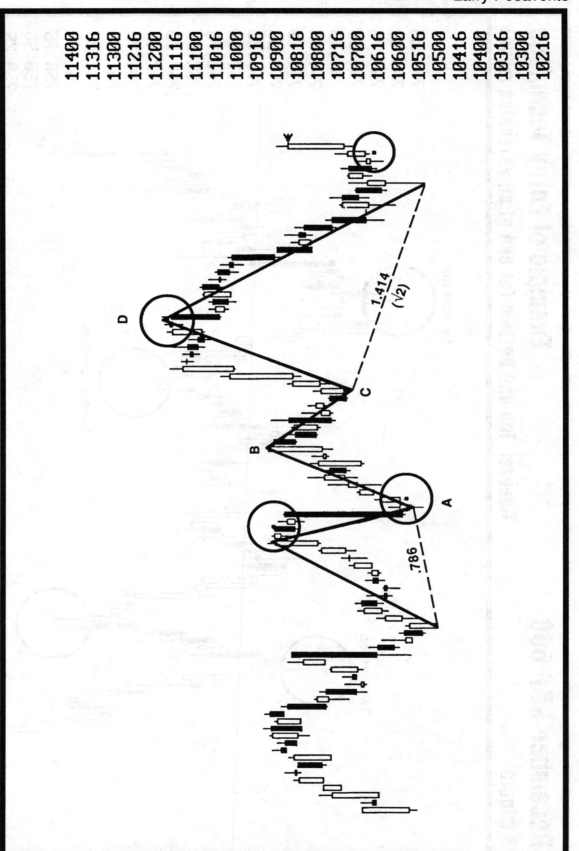

December T-Bonds
Daily

Example of Entry Technique
Doji (at completion of geometric pattern)

It's Different This Time...

The shoeshine boys have computers and are trading stock on the internet

The legendary Joe Kennedy reportedly said that one of the primary reasons he sold his entire stock position in August of 1929 was the fact that the shoeshine boys were giving the stock tips. All one has to do today is get on any one of the hundreds of chat rooms on the internet and you will be totally amazed at what is said. It is so absurd that I'm sure there is not more than a handful of knowledgeable investors/traders contributing on the net. The net surfers seem to thrive on rumor and inuendos.

The internet has brought financial information to the fingertips of any investor—and with lightning speed. Reuter's Instinet is a virtual private cyberspace. No one really seems to understand what really happens there and it is not under the watchful eye of the S.E.C. Volume figures are very hard (if not impossible) to ascertain. Soon after any late breaking news item or earnings report is reported by financial television channel CNBC, the reporter gives the indication that the stock is up or down but with the caveat, "it is very thin trading" on instinet. In my opinion, the use and application of the internet is where television was in the 1950s. It will continue to be an influential factor in Wall Street and around the world. It will only get better. The abuses that occur will, hopefully, be manageable. But, rest assured, there will be abuses—and they will be the feature of the evening news program.

The 1987 Oliver Stone movie, "Wall Street," is the fictitious account of financier Gordon Gekko's shady financial dealing (i.e., trading on inside information). It's ironic that the film was made in 1987 and it starts with Frank Sinatra singing "Fly Me to the Moon."

One sequence in the movie depicts Gordon Gekko talking on the phone with the eager young broker, Bud Fox. Gekko tells the hopeful protege to buy up Teldar stock. He then tells Fox to call the *Wall Street Chronicle* (fictional newspaper) and ask for extension 197. "When the man answers," he says, "tell him 'Blue Horseshoe loves Teldar' and then hang up the phone."

Gordon Gekko has now taken a backseat to the financial news rooms and cyberspace. *Money Magazine* had an article in the June 1998 issue relating how the internet surfets operate.

I spent several trading hours in a level II NASDAQ trading room. They specialize in Small Order Execution System (S.O.E.S.) trading. Traders typically trade 500-1000 shares of stock looking for profits of eighths and quarters, trading 50-100 times per day. Traders in the room have access to about 20 monitors (21-inch color) that give current bids/ask on any stock and the amounts offered. It is a simple process of clicking a mouse button to enter a trade and receive instant confirmation. As soon as the stock moves up a quarter point, the mouse button clicks again and the trader has taken a one-quarter point profit (1000 shares x $.25 = $250, less a $15 commission). The more he trades, the less commission he pays. On the day I was observing, the Stock Market was very strong in all sectors and very few stocks were down. Just before the opening, CNBC's Squak Box program announced that Platinum Entertainment was going to offer music tapes and CDs on the internet. One of the traders, a young man in his early 20s, dressed in a tank top and shorts, stood up and shouted, "Blue Horseshoe loves PTET." The huge entertainment television had the information being released and the sound was turned up very loud. The energy level in the room was approching Super mBowl levels. PTET closed at $7.50/share on July 14th with average an daily volume of 45,000 shares. It opened at $8.50/share. As soon as the stock hit $9/share, the noise level in the room eploded. Mouse buttons clicked as the traders bought. PTET moved staright up to $11/share in the next five minutes. A young Oriental woman in her late 20s proudly stated that she had five profitable trades during that run. The stock stopped going up in the next 15 minutes and fell back to $9.75/share. Noise in the room had dropped to near normal levels. PTET suddenly jumped $1.50/share to go above $11. The whole process was repeated again. All the traders bought as the stock quickly moved to $13/share which is the high of the day. Now the excitement levels are thunderous. Some of the traders were still buying, but most of those trades are breakevens or losses. These were all day trades. Subsequently, PTET fell back to $8/share over the next few days. The play was over—at least for then!

Source Media was the next stock that came into play. CNBC once again announced that the internet company had some announcement pending—a potential buy out candidate! SCRM opened at $21 and moved to $25 in the first two hours of trading, but it went sideways for about an hour at $24/share. In an instant, the stock exploded and in ten minutes it was trading at $30/share. Volume was about 20 times normal, running at over six million shares. The large screen television flashed a news announcement on Source Media! NASDAQ had halted trading in SRCM pending an investigation. The stock had sold off to $25 just before trading was halted. After a two-hour halt, trading was resumed! No announcement from NASDAQ was forthcoming. The stock shot up from its reopening price at $30 ($5 higher than before it was halted). It went to $39/share in the next ten minutes with only an occasional downtick. Only a handful of the traders in the office were involved in the frenzied buying spree. The stock subsequently dropped back to $20/share.

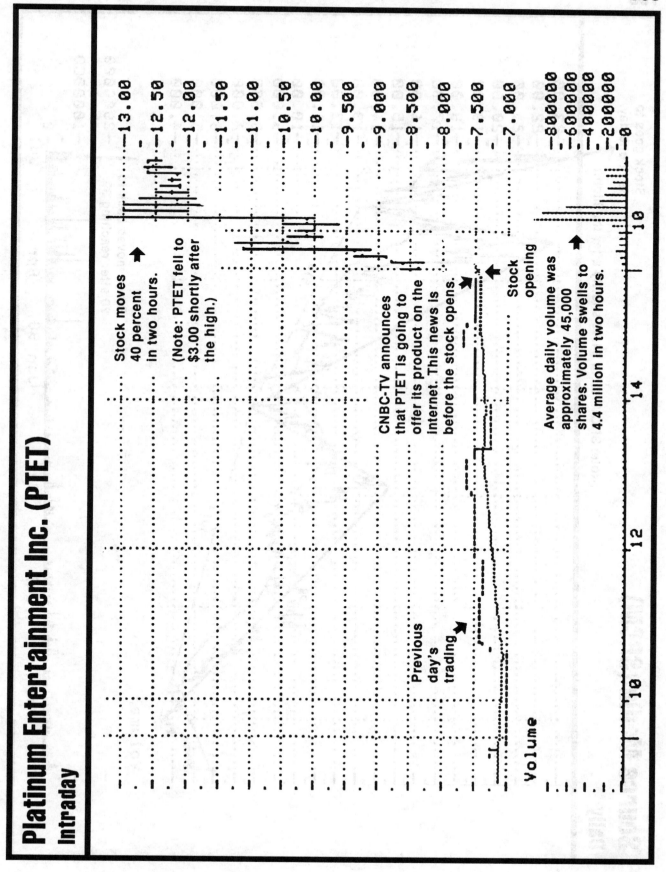

Source Media (SRCM)
Daily

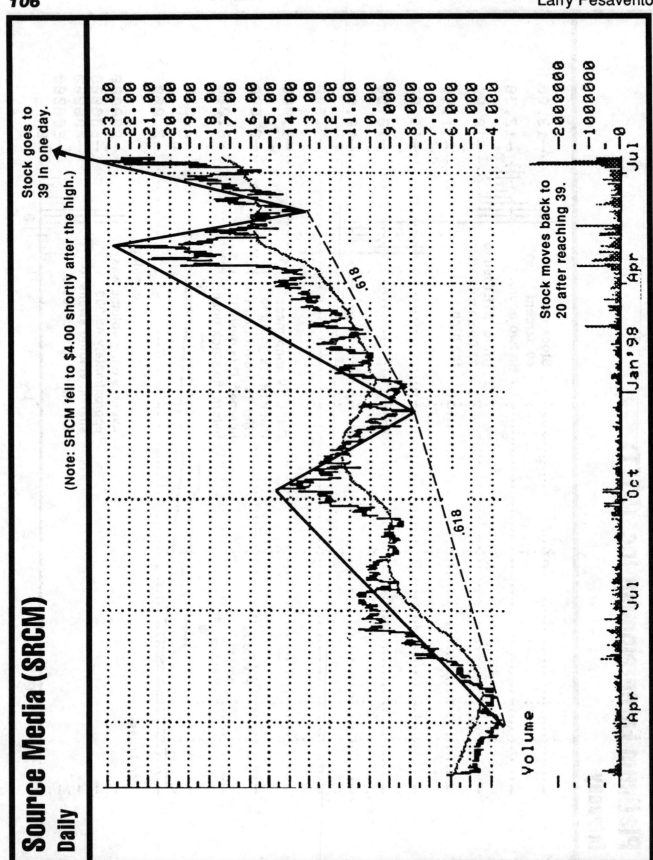

Stock goes to 39 in one day.

(Note: SRCM fell to $4.00 shortly after the high.)

Stock moves back to 20 after reaching 39.

.618

.618

Volume

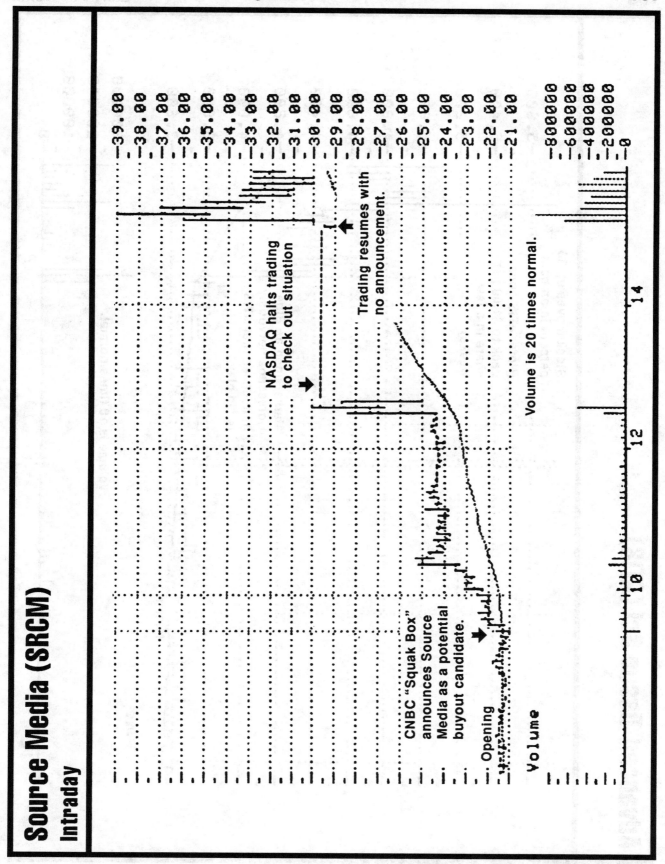

Source Media (SRCM)
Intraday

NASDAQ halts trading
to check out situation

Trading resumes with
no announcement.

CNBC "Squak Box"
announces Source
Media as a potential
buyout candidate.

Opening

Volume is 20 times normal.

Volume

Advanced Tissue Sci (ATIS)

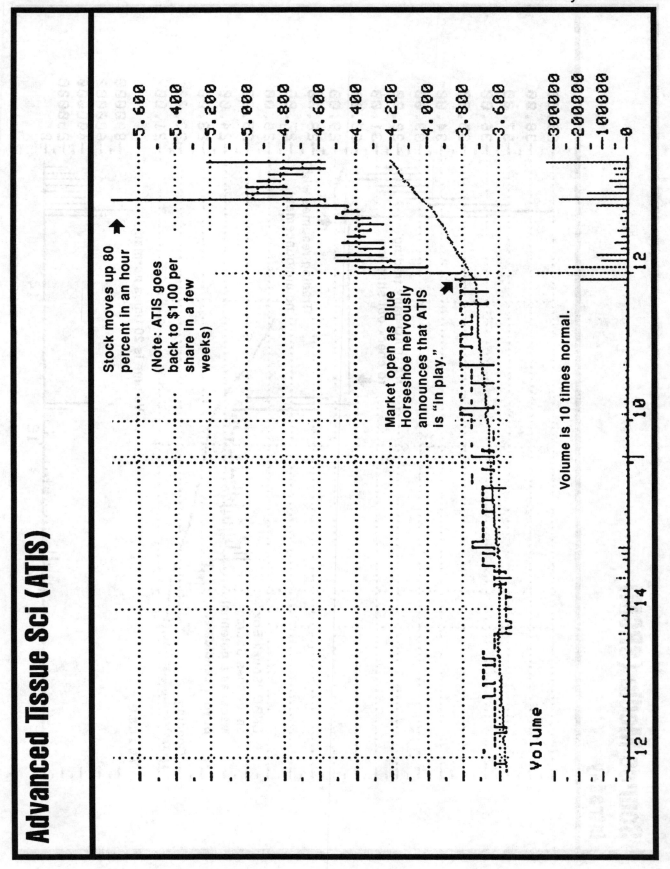

Stock moves up 80 percent in an hour

(Note: ATIS goes back to $1.00 per share in a few weeks)

Market open as Blue Horseshoe nervously announces that ATIS is "in play."

Volume

Volume is 10 times normal.

Advanced Tissue Sciences was mentioned on CNBC's Squak Box before the opening. Blue Horseshoe shouted that ATIS was in play. The chart of ATIS popped up on the large color monitors around the trading floor. Traders anxiously awaited the opening of the stock market. Advanced Tissue opened at just under $4/share and moved to $5.50/share in less than an hour. None of the traders had lost money. Euphoria reigned supreme.

Mindspring Enterprises, one of the few internet stocks that are making money, was rumored to be a potential buyont candidate. But, there was not the same electricity or energy in the trading room as there was with the previous "Blue Horseshoe plays." Then it hit me: This was a very high-priced issue and the trading firm did not allow undermarginal accounts to trade heavily. Mindspring opened higher and immediately moved ten points higher. On a percentage basis, this was a very small move on such a high-priced stock.

One of my most vivid memories of the early 1970s was waiting in line to get gas for the cars. The lines were long and everyone was impatient. It was during one of these encounters that I heard on the car radio that the price of a New York City taxicab medallion exceeded the price of a seat on the New York Stock Exchange (approximately $250,000). As a broker at Drexel, I was well aware that you could not get anyone to buy *any* stock after the last bear market of 1973-74. Real estate and commodities were the biggest games in town.

Now it is 1998 and there are more mutual funds (by a large margin) than there are stocks listed at the New York Stock Exchange! Financial Radio and television programs are everywhere and broadcast 24 hours a day. The *Wall Street Journal* and *Barrons* are three times the thickness of the same publications in the 1970s! *Investor's Business Daily* has been a wel-

come addition to the financial community. The average daily volume on the NYSE regularly exceeds 500 million shares. I can remember a time in 1969, at the Walston & Co. office in San Luis Obispo, California, when the market traded over five million shares in one day. One of the physicians in town sold a block of American South African ADRs (50,000 shares) and we watched it cross the Bunko-Ramo broad tape in the office. We all cheered!

The stocks of that era that were the newsmakers were International Chemical and Nuclear, Computer Science, Memorex and National Video. Computer Sciences was particularly interesting because I had met the founder, Fletcher Jones, in Solvang, California and he told me the computer age was just starting. I had the "inside" information in 1969. Jones was killed a few short years later as he tried to land his private jet at the Solvang airport on a foggy night. He landed at the foot of a small mountain. This mountain would later become famous as the the site of Nancy and Ronald Regan's Western White House. Native Chumash Indians refer to the small mountain as *camino de cielo*—the road to heaven.

Returning to the current "mania" in the internet stocks, Maria Bartaromo, one of my favorites on CNBC, was interviewing one of the members of the NYSE. This is a a regular feature of CNBC programming. On this particular interview, Miss Bartaromo asked the trader what internet stocks he liked. This was on a day when most all stocks were higher, but the internet stocks were flying. His rsponse was something like, "Pizza.com looks interesting." Maria took the bait and said that she wasn't familiar with Pizza.com, but why did he like it? The trader, embarrassed by his playful joke, immediately tried to assure her that he was only joking. She sheepishly ac-

Mindspring Enterprises (MSPG)

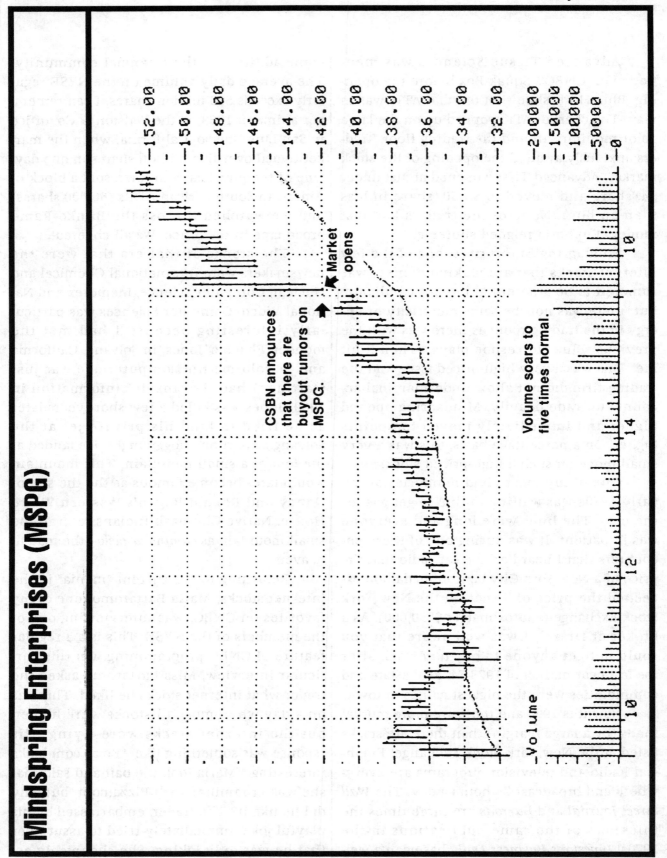

Market opens

CSBN announces
that there are
buyout rumors on
MSPG.

Volume soars to
five times normal.

Volume

knowledged the prank. Anything with .com in its name was in vogue on this day on Wall Street. This is just one example of the ludicrous stories that propel worthless stocks higher and higher. Thirty-plus years of studying every bull and (bear?) market since the tulip mania to the Florida Land Boom makes this observation valid.

Fredrick Lewis Allen's book, Only Yesterday (Bantam 1946), is a vivid account of the 1919-1932 period of the economic and moral aspects of the quality of living in the United States. Virtually no one reading this book was alive or trading stocks in that era. But the big bull gasped it's last breath on September 3rd, 1929. Ten weeks later (in early November), the Stock Market had dropped 50 percent. A rally would then take stocks up 50 percent the old high in April 1930!

There is an unusual company name that pops up in both the current stock market era and the 1929 era. Cable and Wireless was one of the growth stocks in the early 1920s. It sure had a great story—communication (radio, telephone) was the thing of the future. By the mid 1930s, the stock had gone into oblivion and was worthless. Every morning on CNBC they report on the European stock markets. These markets have far surpassed the United States in percentage gains during the last three years. And you will probably be surprised to learn that one of the big speculative plays on the London Stock Exchange is none other than a new version of Cable and Wireless. I wonder if history will be kinder to this company.

Stocks that have already gone through a catharsis in the 1990s are Western Digital Corporation, off 80 percent of its highs; Quarterdack, $38 to 62¢ per share; Iomega, lost 90 percent of its value; Micro Technology, lost 80 percent of its value. There are many others. It has always intrigued me that over 85 percent of the professional mutual fund managers cannot beat the returns of the S&P 500 Index.

As I follow the stock market actively (seven days a week), several things pop out that give me cause for "grave" concern:

1. The Gross Domestic Product was 89 percent of the stock market in 1929. In 1998 it is 130 percent. Once stocks drop, consumption will drop because investors will have less assets.

2. The volume of these paper stocks is well over 100 times that of the 1974—the last time we saw a bear market.

3. The expansion of credit and credit cards is beyond ludicrous. The rates these banks charge used to be called usuary and it was a felony.

4. It seems that most of the CNBC investment stars were still in grade school during the crash of 1987. They have no concept of what a bear market can do. And they all are trained to think long term.

5. Major economic upheavals have already occured in Japan, Southeast Asia, Korea and Russia. Should this economic depression cast its pall over China, it would place one-half of the world in a depression.

6. The money has poured into the

stock mark in the last 25 years. Since 1990, it has been a deluge. They all say that "they are in for the long haul." But, that will not be the case. They will panic, they will cease to invest, they will pull what's left from their accounts. Another bottom will form and another generation will begin to play the game.

The 1929 Bull Market

Stock	Opening Price 3/3/28	High Price 9/3/29
American Can	77	181 7/8
American Telephone & Telegraph	179 1/2	304
Anaconda Copper	54 1/2	131 1/2
General Electric	128 3/4	396 1/4
General Motors	139 3/4	72 3/4
Montgomery Ward	132 3/4	137 7/8
New York Central	160 1/2	256 3/8
Radio	94 1/2	101
Union Carbide & Carbon	145	137 7/8
United ßtates Steel	138 1/8	261 3/4
Westinghouse E. & M.	91 5/8	289 7/8
Woolworth	180 3/4	100 3/8
Electric Bond & Share	89 3/4	186 3/4

Source: *Only Yesterday*, Frederick Lewis Allen

The stocks listed above illustrate the last push upward in stocks during 1928-1929. Most of these stocks doubled in price in 18 months, much like we have seen in 1998. What is interesting about these stocks is that they dropped 90 percent in value over the next four years. After the April 1930 rally, Radio Corp. was reorganized as RCA Corp., Electric Bond & Share went bankrupt. It would take these stocks over 35 years to recover to the 1928-29 levels.

The Non Random Nature of Chaos Theory

The Tomahawk Neural Network

My introduction into the world of artificial intelligence came about purely by accident. About eight years ago (1992), one of my students called to tell be about a man in Bakersfield, California who had been working on a neural network. I had no idea what a neural network was or how it could be applied to trading. Fortunately for me (and I always seem to be fortunate), my good friend Jim Twentyman and I were sharing a trading house in Pismo Beach, California. Jim's expertise is in numbers and computers and he jumped at the chance to start working with neural networks. Little did he realize that he was taking on a monumental task—one that would go on indefinitely.

The first experience we had with neural nets was amazing, to say the least. The man we would eventually work with sent us a fax one morning indicating that the S&P 500 was going to have a 10 point ($5000) move that day. Now I'm sure most of of you reading this have been a giver or receiver of this type of "boardroom tipsters." I certainly confess to that fact. But this time it was different! Not only did the neural net forecast a huge move in the S&P 500, it also forecast a very large counter trend move shortly after the opening (about one hour). Imagine my elation and surprise when the S&P did exactly as the neural network had predicted. Had I finally stumbled on the infamous "Holy Grail?" Stumbled is a good word to use because, over the course of the next four years, I would almost lose my life

and two very special people in my life because of my dedication to neural networks. You must realize that I am "computer phobic." I know very little about computers and have been afraid to learn anything about them, although I do have sense enough to hire the best to work with me. My fear of computers began in 1970 when I finished my Master of Business Administration. I was offered a job with every major company, except IBM. I had taken a computer test and the recruiter said it was the lowest score at my school. Later, I found out it was a test for software programming, for which I had no interest. But this experience anchored my fear of computers and it has stayed with me for 25 years.

After the first experience with a neural network, Jim and I embarked on our journey to find out what it was all about. Very little was written on the subject and those who knew anything were not talking. Our only source of information was from the gentleman in Bakersfield who sent us the fax predicting the huge move in the S&P.

In the 25-plus years I have been in this business, many incredibly bright people have crossed my path. Dennis Regan was certainly one of the brightest. He was an electrical engineer by trade, obtaining a Ph.D. and working for the United States Navy on the Tomahawk missile. His project was to use a heat-seeking device to make the missile hit its target. For this purpose the Navy employed a neural network. Dennis had been working on a neural network for market analysis for over two years when Jim and I first met him. As it turned out, the first S&P prediction we received, although startling, was not indicative of things to come. Dennis had very little experience in financial matters, especially trading. He was self-taught in all areas of his life. He professed that he knew more than anyone and he really believed it. This later became a great obstacle to any improvements in the neural network. The reasons will be readily apparent later, but first let me explain what happened on the day after the first neural net S&P prediction.

I do a lot of trading. Probably too much, at times. It takes very little to get my interest in a trade. If you can, picture someone at the racetrack giving a tip on a horse that goes off at 50 to one and wins. What will his next tip be? It reminds me of a classic racetrack scam. A man approaches a bettor and shows him his winning ticket (usually $2) on the race that just finished. Little does the bettor know that the scam artist has purchased a ticket on every horse in the race and kept them in separate pockets, pulling out the winning ticket as if by magic. He now sells his information on the next race for an exorbitant price due to his "magic touch." He then disappears into the crowd to find another "dupe." Should the horse win by some miracle, he knows where to find his pigeon. If the horse doesn't win (which is usual) and the dupe accosts him, the scam artist simply says, "That's horse racing—nothing is guaranteed!"

But this time I knew I wasn't at the racetrack when I saw the neural net prediction. Intuition was with me on this one. I have been involved with cycles for many years from linear regression, Fourier analysis and astro-harmonic planetary cycles. One of my favorite quotes from ancient Chinese literature (Lao Tse) is: "When the student is ready, the teacher will appear." As the day of the prediction unfolded I was on the phone with Dennis several times. Fortune was again smiling on me as the S&P opened sharply lower, completing a perfect pattern recognition signal. I bought near the low of the day, and away the S&P went. My excitement level increased in direct proportion to the rising prices of the S&P 500. I remember this trade quite well because, after about two hours, I had made about four points which is more than the average daily trading range. I closed out the trade with a sizable profit and was quite happy. When I told Dennis, his behavior put me in a state of shock! He scolded me for exiting too soon and then he hung up abruptly. It was at this point that I realized he was two French fries short of a Happy Meal. This was not to say he was crazy, he was just eccentric in every phase of his life (and I emphasize every).

Over the next several days, Jim and I talked with Dennis several times each day. This phase of the relationship lasted several weeks. Dennis wanted several thousand dollars a month for his fax predictions. I paid this in cash to him. Part of his eccentricity was his protesting the payment of taxes to the Internal Revenue Service. He had a longstanding dispute with them and owed them over $1 million in interest and penalties. These weeks were very frustrating to me because Dennis was so unreasonable and obstinate. Day after day we listened to the genius and his right-wing philosophies.

I can't recall exactly what happened, but Dennis and I argued about something (probably money) and I decided it was in my own best interests to let Jim communicate with him. I then could listen to the conversations and sit back and laugh about it later with Jim. What I didn't realize until much later was that I had shirked some of the responsibility of working on the project. All I did was pay the money—which was the easiest part! The difficult part was working with Dennis. He was a classic workaholic with paranoid tendencies. He was afraid of the IRS and trusting anyone! As you can imagine, this was a far cry from a perfect working environment. So you ask me the big question: Why didn't I just tell him to take a hike? Believe me when I tell you that it crossed my mind many times. You must remember that Jim Twentyman was handling the day to day combat with Dennis so that pressure was relieved from me. Unfortunately the pressure didn't disappear. It was simply transferred to Jim. Dennis had an unbridled desire to be perfect and this was reflected in his work habits. Many times he would work day after day without sleep, becoming more obstinate as each hour passed. Stress was getting to Jim and it became a very touchy subject. Dennis would sometimes call in the middle of the night wanting Jim's advice or just to talk shop. Classic signs of a depressed genius were everywhere, but when you want something so bad you overlook the obvious. I don't quite remember what triggered Jim's anger, but he finally threw up his hands in disgust and dropped the neural network project right in my lap. In retrospect, he was using his own body's defense mechanism to survive.

Approximately eight or nine months transpired. The money was going down a bottomless black hole. First, there was Dennis' consulting fee (always in cash or gold). Next it was a very expensive ($12,000) personal computer with every bell and whistle imaginable. Of course, the price dropped in half shortly after I purchased the computer and sent it to Dennis. Later it became necessary to buy a work station in order to increase the speed of the neural net—another $20,000. Ironically, I was almost as bad as Dennis in my zeal to find

answers. The difference was that I kept it internally and only those very close to me were aware of what was happening. It wasn't too long when everyone would know what was happening.

A normal trading day for me starts at 4 a.m. checking on the foreign equity markets and the major currencies. It was August 15th, 1992, and over two years of neural network had been completed. I was having a normal day and a student was with me watching me trade. It was a fun day and we were just about finished trading and getting ready to go to lunch. The student commented that I looked a little pale and was soaking wet. Sure enough, he was right. My first response was to assume that I was coming down with the flu—that's the standard response. We decided that I wouldn't go to lunch and I proceeded to go home and take a nap, although I didn't feel ill. However, I was a bit tired. Sleeping for an hour or so refreshed me and I decided to watch the Market Wrap Show on CNBC. We were scheduled to go to the State Fair that evening, but I was too tired. I went to bed around 7 p.m. At 3:30 a.m. I began to make moaning sounds and stumbled into the bathroom. One look in the mirror told me I was in trouble. I had a rapid pulse, my skin color was grayish yellow and I was sweating profusely. Even with my limited medical training I knew it was internal bleeding. Paramedics rushed me to the hospital emergency room and a vascular surgeon greeted me. After X-rays and blood tests, he diagnosed an aneurysm in my esophagus. I had been bleeding internally for several days and I didn't have any clue as to what was happening. Immediately following laser surgery to repair the bleeding, I was placed in intensive care for four days. Supposedly, I was within hours of dying. I had no pain or discomfort at all. The only complaint was fatigue and muscle weakness. Recuperation was very lengthy and required that I only work part time for several months. My general health had been excellent and my physician commented that is probably why I handled the crisis as well as I did. This was my first official hospital visit and it scared me beyond belief. Two months before the incident I took out a health plan. As it turned out, it was my best trade of the year because it saved me $25,000 in out-of-pocket medical expenses. Having been in excellent health up to that time, I assumed I was oblivious to an emergency or an accident. My appreciation of the simple things in life was increased immensely. Several months later I was back in the same work routine, but this time I was very cautious about my health. Ironically, the most vivid memory I had was in the ambulance on the way to the hospital. The paramedic kept telling me we would be at the hospital soon and not to panic. Quite the contrary, I was very peaceful and thought that if this was how death was to be, it was nothing to fear. My children held my closest thoughts as well as my fiancée, Benida. Without her I would surely have died. I will always owe her a debt of gratitude.

Dennis completely changed his relationship with me once I returned to work. He was cordial, patient and understanding. I didn't know at first if he was being genuinely kind or if he had finally realized that all of his supporters had abandoned him because of the difficulty working with him. It became quite apparent that he was truly kind and caring.

Now that I was working with Dennis on my own it became necessary to travel to his home in Bakersfield. Several trips were made to deliver computers and others to discuss how to proceed with the neural net research. The trip across the desert took about 2 1/2 hours. Upon arriving I was totally amazed at what I

found. Dennis and his wife and two small children were living in a small three room house. And I do mean a small house. My office was much bigger. It was incredibly messy, with Pepsi cans and empty potato chip bags on the floor. The scene did not change on subsequent visits. You must imagine how it felt to leave a $20,000 computer in this environment, especially with Dennis' background as an IRS protester. But I now felt comfortable with him and knew he trusted me.

Dennis was a huge man of 6'3" and over 300 pounds. He was totally bald and kept his head cleanly shaved—a very imposing figure. His office was in an 8x10-foot room with wall to wall computers and a small cot which he slept on. There was a huge steel safe five feet high with double door—the kind you used to see in Western movies. I never knew what was in the safe because, when I asked, he would change the subject abruptly. He always had an open can of Pepsi and a big bag of potato chips handy. Exercise was out of the question because it took time out from the neural network research. I really did not like to visit him because there was no place to sit down in his office, so I planned trips only when necessary.

The next few months ran smoothly. Dennis' demands for more money abated. As long as he had a steady income each month he was happy. It enabled him to provide for his family and research neural networks. When I first met Dennis he was managing a $100,000 commodity account in which he received 25 percent of the profits. In the first three months, the profits were over $250,000. The client then stopped trading, closed the account and moved to Costa Rica. Later, Dennis told me that the man was also an IRS protester. Dennis found another client with $50,000. It was my good friend, Dr. Jim Elder. Jim is an M.D. specializing in Pathology. We had been friends about three years at that time and, on one of his visits to Pismo Beach, he was very impressed at what the neural networks could do. Immediately after Jim opened his account I went to Mexico for a vacation. During that week Dennis lost over half of the account. His trading was wild and erratic and had nothing to do with the neural networks. There was no money management strategy of any kind. Shock could not adequately describe how I felt. I knew what Dennis had tried to accomplish. He assumed that he could trade the same way that he did in the other account. What happened to him has happened to many other traders in the past. His first few trades were quite large and incurred losses. Not catastrophic losses, but substantial enough to hurt. He then tried to make the money back on the next trade. Each time he would fail to put in a stop loss, hoping for the market to turn around and save him. This reminds me of one of Mark Douglass' favorite quotes from his book The Disciplined Trader—"Don't expect the market to save you, you must save yourself."

Dennis lost more than 80 percent of the $50,000 in just a few short weeks. It was impossible to talk to him about his trading. He thought he knew more than anyone. Finally, he became paranoid that the brokers in the pits were "picking off" his two and three lot trades. This was totally absurd, but he refused to listen. Dr. Elder's account was down to just a few thousand dollars when Dennis decided to quit trading due to total frustration and lack of confidence. It would prove to be the best thing for all of us later on because he was able to return to his research and it released him from the stress of trading. Dennis and Jim Elder became friends and spoke often on the telephone about the neural network research. Jim Elder came to Pismo Beach to visit me several times each year. On one of these visits

in December of 1992 he mentioned that he wanted to visit Dennis. We drove together to Bakersfield one foggy morning. Jim was also startled by the living conditions of Dennis. Since only two people could be in the room at any one time, I decided to go to a movie while Dennis and Jim talked computers. It was the smartest thing to do because the two of them knew computers and I would have only been in the way. There was not room to get in the way! After the visit, Jim and I drove home. As we drove across the desolate stretch of desert, Jim told me that only a handful of people had the intelligence of Dennis. He was a true genius! That helped explain his bizarre behavior to a great extent.

As the Christmas holidays approached, Dennis and I focused our attention on how to market the neural net program. The program was copyrighted by me under the name "Tomahawk." Tomahawk was chosen for two reasons. First, it had the cutting precision of a tomahawk. Second, the principles of vibration and harmonics in the formulas were similar to those in the neural net software used by the Tomahawk missiles. They are by no means secret formulas because they are used by electrical engineers frequently. Even though the software program was not perfected, it certainly was better than anything I had ever seen in my 27 years in the commodity business. Most of the improvements would come at a later date.

This closes the opening chapter of the neural net saga. Little did I realize how my life was going to change over the next few weeks. The ancient Chinese adage, "That which doesn't destroy me shall make me stronger," was certainly coming my way without any forewarning.

Bells began to toll for me soon after Christmas 1992, one of the most enjoyable holidays I can remember. I was able to visit with many old friends, and especially with my two daughters. My health was excellent, but this was not unexpected because I have always been in good shape physically. Dennis had called me early one morning and it was quite apparent that he was sick with a horrible case of the flu, complete with fever, sore throat and lung congestion. We agreed that he should rest and recuperate before we proceeded any further. This was really the appropriate strategy primarily because his health was so important, but secondarily because he had not taken a day off in the three and a half years I knew him. He remained bedridden over the next few days. Meiko, his wife, and I kept in daily contact on the progress of his health. Antibiotics were used to protect against pneumonia. For a short time he appeared to be recovering. Then his health took a turn for the worse and he had to be rushed to the hospital for admittance. Now I was really worried! Dennis weighed over 300 pounds and never exercised, a deadly combination. The doctor came back with news that Dennis had a serious heart problem and would have to lead an even more sedentary life and reduce outside stress. He would be a cardiac invalid! All of us who were friendly with Dennis were very sad, but not surprised. The compulsive work habits and the absence of any diet/exercise program had taken its toll. The cardiologist assigned to Dennis wanted to do bypass surgery. Risk in surgery is always present, but with his weight and medical history, increased risk was apparent. A cardiac catheterization test was ordered and it verified our worst fears—Dennis' heart was about 25 percent functional. Then catastrophic news came. As the physician was removing the cardiac catheter, Dennis had a heart attack. His heart stopped and had to be restarted, but he made it through.

Over the next several days he improved dramatically and his doctors were amazed at his recovery and overall health and stamina. He was scheduled to be released in a few days. Everyone was excited. He then died quietly in his sleep the night before his release. Later, I was informed that only the immediate family knew his days were numbered and they did not want Dennis to know it was his time to go. It is not the choice I would have made, but it was not my choice to make. He was cremated the next day by his family.

Meiko called me to see if I could pick up my computers and if I wanted to buy any of Dennis' office supplies. My trip to his home was very sad. I had grown to really care for Dennis and his family and it was now over. I was also facing a dilemma. How was I going to continue the neural net project? Computers were foreign to me and I had a phobia of them. Jim Elder stepped in to help me. Without his help I would have abandoned the project at that moment. How was I going to handle a project as computer intensive as a neural network?

Cal Poly State University was located in San Luis Obispo and was blessed with an excellent computer science department. Placing an ad for a computer jock was one of my better decisions. Offering to pay $3 per hour above the going hourly rate inundated me with applicants. I finally settled on a computer science major, Chris Nichol, in his junior year. Chris was very energetic, capable and personable. I think he would have worked for me for free. With Chris' help and Jim Elder's support, we were able to get the neural net working in about a month. Jim had begun to make changes in the program that dramatically increased the accuracy of the neural nets. Chris had little experience with financial markets, but he learned quickly what we needed. It became necessary to purchase a work station in order to process the data each day. Memory was not our problem—the speed of the calculations were the problem. I bought the best available computer. Why not get the best for something with as much potential as our program?

The Comdex computer show was in Las Vegas so Chris and I traveled together to buy a work station. I had never seen so many people in one place (except for the Indianapolis 500 Motor Speedway). There were over 250,000 people registered. It is the biggest single event of the year for Las Vegas convention resorts. Everything you could ever imagine for computers is there: Companies are showcasing their research and development capabilitie, new products are being introduced, orkshops are held hourly, technical support people are everywhere to answer questions and demonstrate their products. It would take three full days to go through the exhibits and that's not leaving much time to stop and chat. Meals and rooms in Las Vegas are at premium levels. You must have reservations at any of the good restaurants in order to be served. It is a classic zoo-like scenario for the entire week of Comdex.

Chris and I spent one day going to the companies that offered what we needed. I had no idea what the technicians were describing to Chris on what we needed versus what they offered. I might as well have been in China because the language was so foreign. The next two days I wandered about the exhibits trying to learn anything I could by osmosis. All it did was confuse me even more. My phobia of computers was apparent once again and it was intensifying. But there were neat little gifts such as T-shirts, tool kits and posters that I collected. My rationale was that I was out to get something for all the money I was spending. I did purchase a trackball keyboard system with a built-in mouse that is very helpful in my day-to-day charting. Chris spent all of his time going back and forth from vendor to vendor asking every conceivable question about their products and how it might fit our needs. Finally, we had exactly what we wanted and ordered it for 30 day delivery, because part of the computer had to be customized for our specific purpose.

The computer was delivered in February 1994. It increased the speed of training time by a factor of five. We needed this speed to make three- to five-day projections. Having such price and time projections would increase the flexibility of our neural net, particularly as it relates to the option markets. For example, if the neural net forecast is predicting a substantial price move in the next three days, a volatility spread could be instituted. Buying both a put and a call would insure you would be in the market when it starts its move. One would be worthless, but the other would have increased in value. Conversely, if the neural net indicated a flat market over the next three to five days, you could sell a put and sell a call, gathering the premium on both sides of the trade. As 1994 is drawing to a close, we have not made any significant progress to make these three to five day projections. Our problem is one of time and manpower. Chris returned to finish his college education so it was necessary to replace him. Dr. Pat now enters the picture.

Dr. Patrick McGuire is a 27-year-old Ph.D. in applied mathematics from the University of Arizona. He is extremely well qualified and very interested in neural networks. Patrick has been working with me over the last six months trying to solve this problem. We are making progress, but it is much slower than I would like to see. For the first few months it seemed that I was only buying more memory and extra gadgets for the computer. The daily neural nets work so well I frequently wonder if I should be satisfied with what I have and leave it at that. There must come a time when you finally stop pouring money into a project due to the concept of diminishing returns. Whatever happens from this point forward is not as important as what has happened so far. The Tomahawk neural network software system demonstrates that speculative markets are not totally random. Within the chaos of the market, vibrations are identifiable patterns that reappear over and over again. Each of these patterns brings a trading opportunity. It is the responsibility of the trader to determine which pattern is present and the risk involved. Risk

is the only thing we can control in a trade! No one can tell us with 100 percent accuracy what is going to happen next.

He who knows not
what he risks—risks all!

Risk!!
The perception becomes real!

LBH

Order Out of Chaos

To give you an idea of the harmonic nature of the markets, I'd like to walk you through a little mathematical example. Select any two numbers between one and infinity ∞. (Let's use 297 and 11,492.) Now let's go through the following calculations.

	297	
	+11,492	add the sum to the next number
1	+11,789	
2	+23,281	
3	+35,070	
4	+58,351	
5	+93,421	
6	+151,772	
7	+245,193	
8	+396,965	

245,193/396,965 = .618 (The Golden Ratio) of the Fibonacci Summation Series

Once you reach the eighth harmonic you get the .618 ratio and it stays there for infinity. This is just one of the many examples of the mathematical riddles inherent in the ratios of sacred geometry. Each day the Tomahawk neural network system starts with two random two-minute time bars and then proceeds to scan 20,000 interactions in search of the appropriate pattern.

When the strike of a hawk breaks the body of its prey, it is because of timing.

—Sun Tzu, The Art of War

Tony Robbins lists seven beliefs in success that all successful people use in their quest for excellence. Success belief number four really describes my relationship with the Tomahawk neural network. Number 4 states: "It is not necessary to understand everything in order to be able to use everything." It would be about as easy as teaching brain surgery to you in a few pages as trying to explain a neural network. But here it is in layman's terms with the least amount of technical jargon.

Machines that think, that use reason and logic to solve problems, have long been the ultimate fantasy of science fiction writers. Now it is the computer scientists who are poking about the fundamental concepts of how the mind works in an effort to develop programs that imitate the brain's behavior and actually think.

In 1955 Herbert Simon of Carnegie-Mellon University developed a program that worked out simple REM (Rapid Eye Movement). Since then, research in theoretical mathematics, coupled with advances in microtechnology developed for the space program, has led to development of the science of Artificial Intelligence. A driving force in this field is neural network technology, a new class of computing that uses from hundreds to hundreds of thousands of simulated neurons, all connected to one another, to perform analyses and draw conclusions in a primitive imitation of how the human brain functions.

These simulated neurons, or nodes, are simple processors wired so that each one can communicate with or send signals to a group of other nodes. This internal exchange of information teaches the network relationships or associations. When a single node is given an input data point A it responds with an output result B. "Training" a neural network means presenting it with a series of input-output pairs, or associations, called "facts."

The output portion of a fact is referred to as a training pattern. Neural networks are trained by presenting them with a set of facts over and over!

It takes over 500,000 iterations for a single analysis. Every time a neuron reads an input it calculates what it determines the answer, or output, should be. Outputs from one neuron are used as inputs for another.

Although individual neurons, or logic points, may each only work on a small portion of a total problem, collectively this training process is repeated until the network uses all of the "facts" correctly, meaning the final result or "solution" is within an acceptable group of parameters, and the problem is solved. In the brain this process is known as parallel distributed processing.

It is the job of the programmer to properly define the problem and select the appropriate set of facts for the network to analyze in order to get a "correct" answer.

Neural networks as an analytical tool have a number of advantages over standard computing. They can process a great deal of information virtually instantaneously and simultaneously, making them much faster than conventional programming.

Nets are also more reliable because they distribute data throughout the entire system for processing. This means most of the net can still function if a few nodes break down, or some of the inputs are questionable. This "graceful degradation" allows analysis if enough input passes are made in the training.

Perhaps the neural nets' greatest advantage is their ability to generalize. Training teaches the nets to recognize more than just the specific examples or patterns they have already seen. They can also recognize patterns that resemble the training examples and interpolate and manipulate them as well.

These attributes make neural network theory a logical choice for commodity analysis. One of the most promising applications uses cycle theory data to determine output patterns that define timing points to identify trend changes in commodity price movements.

The Tomahawk© neural network program is incredibly complex. The idea began with a neural network system used by the United States Navy in offensive mechanisms in the Tomahawk heat seeking missile. The missiles had to differentiate between submarines, large whales, rock formations and other large oceanic forms. The harmonic vibrations illustrated by the Doppler effect give a simplified explanation of how the missile operates. The feedback vibrations of a submarine are characteristically different from any other object. Wave vibrations in speculative markets also have identifiable patterns. These wave patterns can be categorized. Armed with this information, the neural net forecasts the next day's market forecast. This is why I think the Tomahawk works so well: 1) Markets are nonlinear; 2) markets are chaotic, but within the chaos are predictable patterns; 3) The patterns

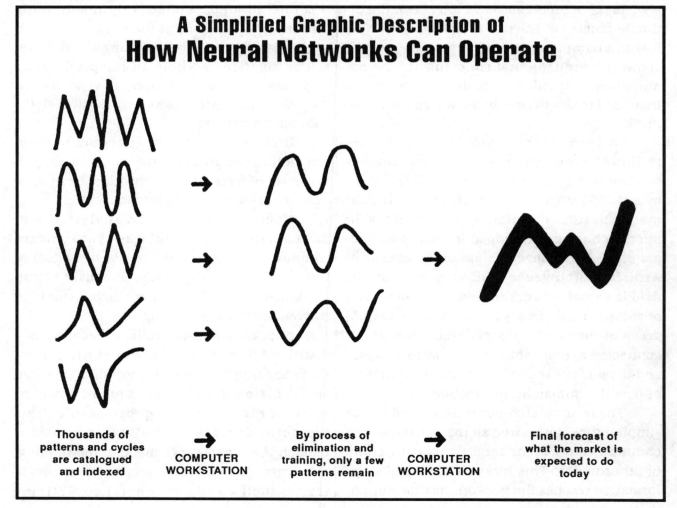

A Simplified Graphic Description of
How Neural Networks Can Operate

Thousands of patterns and cycles are catalogued and indexed → **COMPUTER WORKSTATION** → **By process of elimination and training, only a few patterns remain** → **COMPUTER WORKSTATION** → **Final forecast of what the market is expected to do today**

are repetitive in both price and time; 4) The vibrations and harmonics are predictable within certain limits, but they can be indexed and categorized; 5) Time and price are the only vehicles in the input data.

Those of you familiar with Excel can appreciate what 50 to 100 spread sheets would look like with each connected to the other and some overlapping. Then you would have a brief glimpse of the very basics of simple neural networks. The Tomahawk was developed to predict what would happen the next day in any liquid speculative market. This holds true for listed stocks, bonds or any popular investment vehicle that is actively traded. It has been tested on New York Stock Exchange stock favorites such as IBM, Eastman Kodak, Coca-Cola and most of the Dow Jones stocks. Active NASDAQ stocks were tested with positive results. The Tomahawk does not work with illiquid stocks or bonds. Nor does it work with IPOs (Initial Price Offerings) because of the lack of any back data and low liquidity.

The process that the Tomahawk goes through to forecast the next day's trend is started automatically at the close of the S&P 500 at the Chicago Mercantile Exchange (4:15 p.m. CST). All two minute price bars for the past 30 days are saved; the oldest date is dropped automatically. Macro keys process the data. It is then transferred to the neural network computer by floppy disk. After three hours of hard work, the neural net is finished and the predictions are ready for the next day. I then transfer the floppy disk from the neural net computer back to the trading computer which has on-line price quotes from all major exchanges.

The neural net forecasts are then laid over on-line price bars. Now it is in the trader's hands. He must look at the comparison of the actual market versus the forecast of the neural net. If the patterns match two questions must be asked: 1) Is the price pattern matching the neural network? 2) Can I afford to take the risk in the trade? If the answer to both of these questions is yes, then the trade must be taken. The reason it must be taken is simple: no one knows which trades will be profitable. We are operating in a world of probabilities. Losses are as natural as breathing! If you cannot take a loss, or find it difficult to admit you are wrong, then find another career. It will save you a great deal of money and, more importantly, it will increase your chances for peace of mind and happiness.

The segment of computer science focused on problem solving comes under the branch of artificial intelligence, commonly referred to as A.I. by its supporters. Within the realm of A.I.'s kingdom are several substates. Here are only a few of them:

A. Expert systems—These programs try to mimic the human brain by providing solutions automatically when a whole series of questions are answered. The sequence takes the form of "what-if" questioning.

B. Case-based reasoning—Here all past problems and solutions are indexed and classified. They are stored in memory and will be recalled when the appropriate solution is indicated or repeated.

C. Chaotic systems—Nonlinear differential equations are used to find the predictable patterns within the chaos. This is particularly suited to financial markets because it may alert the trader to an impending change in market dynamics (i.e., trend change, increased volatility).

D. Fuzzy logic—This mimics the human brain by its ability to make judgments. These judgments are then classified and stored for use in the next set of problems/solutions.

The Doppler Effect

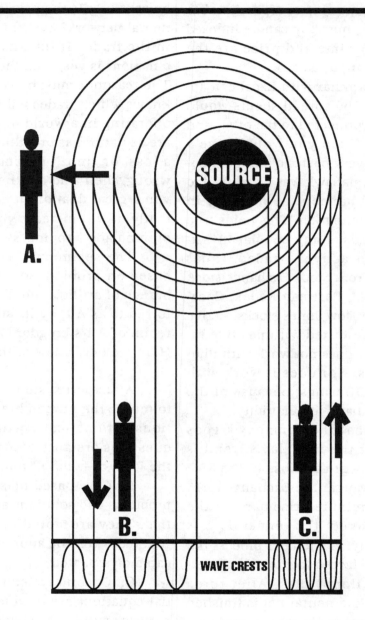

The Doppler Effect is a change in the observed frequency of sound or light resulting from the motion of a source or observer.

Successive wave crests emitted by a stationary source in all directions approach any stationary observer (**A**) at a constant distance, or wavelength, behind each other and at a constant frequency.

If the source moves away from an observer or the observer moves away from the source (**B**), the waves seem to be drawn out to longer wavelengths and are received at a lower frequency.

If the source approaches an observer or the observer moves toward the source (**C**), the waves are crowded together; appearing shorter in wavelength and follow each other at a higher frequency

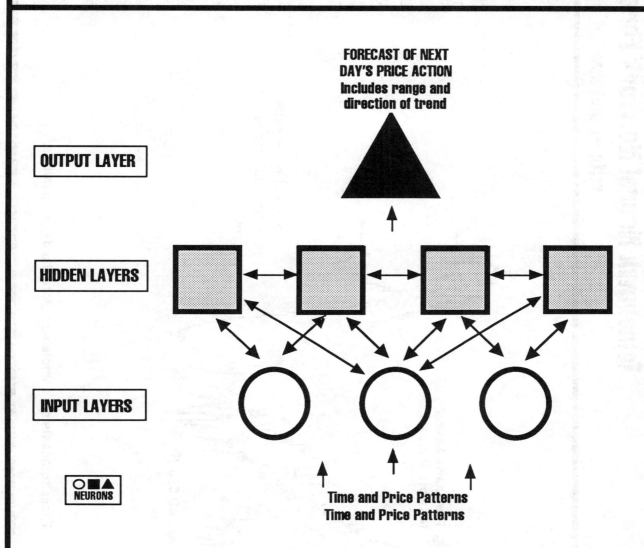

Schematic of Tomahawk© Neural Network

FORECAST OF NEXT DAY'S PRICE ACTION Includes range and direction of trend

OUTPUT LAYER

HIDDEN LAYERS

INPUT LAYERS

◯ ▪ ▲
NEURONS

Time and Price Patterns
Time and Price Patterns

My theory of market dynamics is based on the principle that markets react to two basic emotions: fear and greed. Through a complex system of patterns and cycles, all very liquid speculative markets behave in the same manner. In doing so, they can be quantified, thereby permitting estimation of the amplitude and duration of these cycles. Greed is dominant at cycle tops and fear is predominant at market bottoms.

That all markets behave the same way over time can be proven easily. If you were to take an active chart and randomly select a period of time, then remove the x and y axis headings, what remains is a bar chart. No one can tell you what the chart is describing—over time, all charts will look the same.

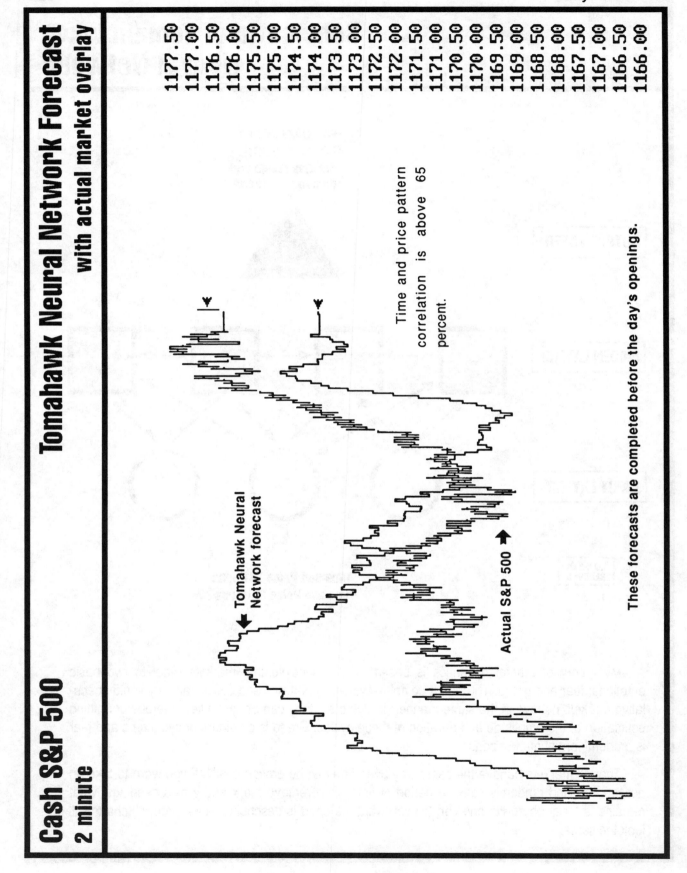

Cash S&P 500
2 minute

Tomahawk Neural Network Forecast
with actual market overlay

Tomahawk Neural Network forecast

Actual S&P 500

Time and price pattern correlation is above 65 percent.

These forecasts are completed before the day's openings.

1177.50
1177.00
1176.50
1176.00
1175.50
1175.00
1174.50
1174.00
1173.50
1173.00
1172.50
1172.00
1171.50
1171.00
1170.50
1170.00
1169.50
1169.00
1168.50
1168.00
1167.50
1167.00
1166.50
1166.00

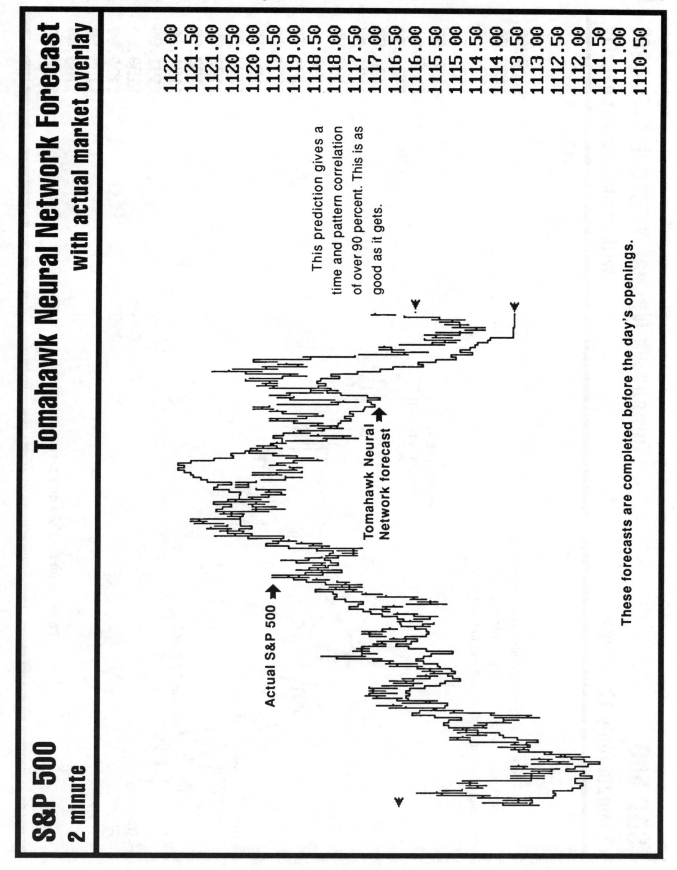

S&P 500
2 minute

Tomahawk Neural Network Forecast
with actual market overlay

1122.00
1121.50
1121.00
1120.50
1120.00
1119.50
1119.00
1118.50
1118.00
1117.50
1117.00
1116.50
1116.00
1115.50
1115.00
1114.50
1114.00
1113.50
1113.00
1112.50
1112.00
1111.50
1111.00
1110.50

This prediction gives a time and pattern correlation of over 90 percent. This is as good as it gets.

Actual S&P 500

Tomahawk Neural Network forecast

These forecasts are completed before the day's openings.

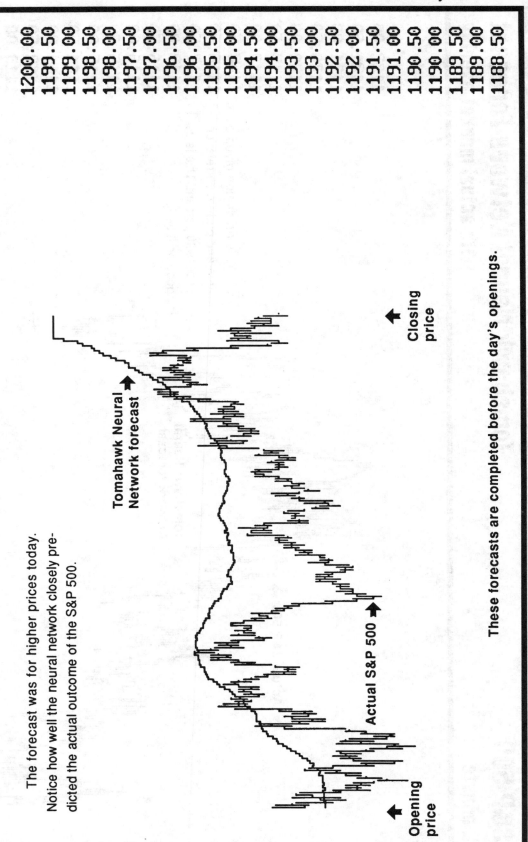

Tomahawk Neural Network Forecast
with actual market overlay

S&P 500
2 minute (July 17, 1998)

The forecast was for higher prices today.
Notice how well the neural network closely pre-
dicted the actual outcome of the S&P 500.

Tomahawk Neural
Network forecast

Actual S&P 500

Opening price

Closing price

These forecasts are completed before the day's openings.

1200.00
1199.50
1199.00
1198.50
1198.00
1197.50
1197.00
1196.50
1196.00
1195.50
1195.00
1194.50
1194.00
1193.50
1193.00
1192.50
1192.00
1191.50
1191.00
1190.50
1190.00
1189.50
1189.00
1188.50

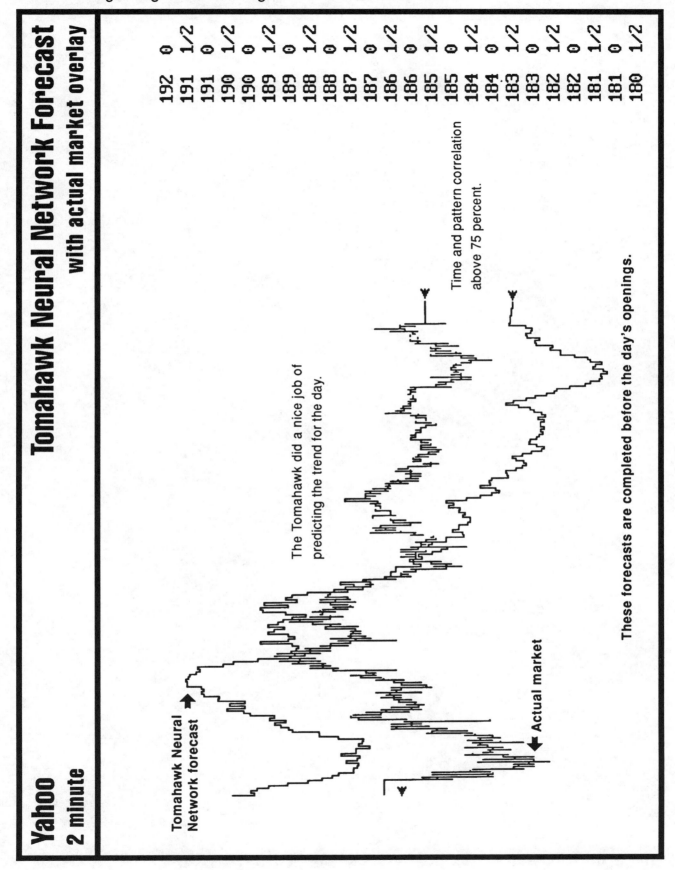

Yahoo
2 minute

Tomahawk Neural Network Forecast
with actual market overlay

192	0
191	1/2
191	0
190	1/2
190	0
189	1/2
189	0
188	1/2
188	0
187	1/2
187	0
186	1/2
186	0
185	1/2
185	0
184	1/2
184	0
183	1/2
183	0
182	1/2
182	0
181	1/2
181	0
180	1/2

Time and pattern correlation above 75 percent.

The Tomahawk did a nice job of predicting the trend for the day.

These forecasts are completed before the day's openings.

Tomahawk Neural Network forecast

Actual market

Appendix I

Description of Gartley "222"

This is the description of the Gartley "222" pattern exactly as it appears on pages 221-222 of Gartley's book, *Profits in the Stock Market.*

One of the Best Trading Opportunities

In the life of those who dabble on Wall street, at some time or another there comes a yearning—"just to buy them right, once, if never again." For those who have patience, the study of top and bottom patterns will provide such an opportunity every now and then—the chance does not arise everyday, but when it does, a worthwhile opportunity, with small risk becomes available.

Figure 27 (A)

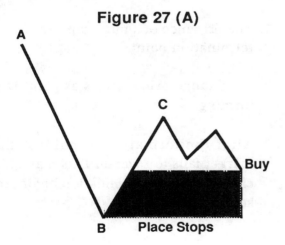

Let us look at Figure 27(A). When, after an intermediate decline in either a bull or a bear market, such as A-B in the diagram, has proceeded for some time, and activity has shown a definite tendency to dry up, indication that liquidation is terminating, a minor rally like B-C sets in, with volume expanding on the upside. And when a minor decline, after cancelling a third to a half of the preceding minor advance (B-C) comes to a halt, with vol-

ume drying up again, a real opportunity is presented to buy stocks, with a stop under the previous low.

In eight out of ten cases wherein each of these specific conditions occurs, a rally, which will provide a worthwhile profit, ensues. In the other two cases, only small losses have to be taken. In trading this formation, the observer is depending upon the probability that either a head-and-shoulders, or double bottom, which are the two reversal patterns which occur most frequently, is developing.

The art in conducting an operation of this kind lies in:

a. Having the patience to wait until a decline of substantial proportions has developed;

b. Observing that all conditions laid down are present;

c. Having the courage to buy just as soon as the minor reaction which tests the bottom shows signs of terminating; and

d. Having the courage to get out with a fair profit (10-20 per cent), or at least protect it with stops.

Hourly charts of the averages, available for guiding the operation, repay the market student for all the efforts he puts into keeping them day after day, when they are of less practical use.

Similar opportunities occasionally de-

velop for that small part of the trading frater-
nity which has the intestinal fortitude and
temperament to sell stocks short. The case in
reverse is laid out in of Figure 27(B).

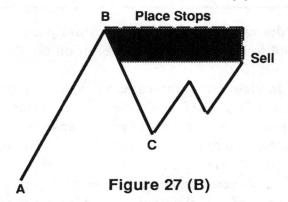

Figure 27 (B)

Gartley's book was written in the 1930s
and things have changed dramatically about
the markets. Not the markets themselves, but
the way they are reported. Communication is
now instantaneous because of the statellite
dishes around the world connected to all the
computer trading desks around the world.
During Gartley's era, the Western Union
tickertape was the method of communciation.
As I wrote that last sentence, I realized that is
how I learned to trade soybeans with Dave
Nelson on his Trans Lux ticker tape.

Thousands of new stocks and commodity
markets have been introduced since Gartley's
time. Most of these are very liquid and easy to
gain access to the chart patterns. This is particularly true for the intraday charts. In this
section of the appendix, I have selected some
intraday charts illustrating these patterns.

Included in teh appendix is the page on
my monitor that shows what commoditites
and stocks I follow. Each has a monthly, daily
and intraday chart pattern. Intraday charts are
2 minutes, 5 minutes, 30 minutes, 60 minutes
as well as a tick chart to record every tick.
This is helpful to gauge whether or not you are
filled on your order and at what price.

As one reads the "222" pattern described
by H. M. Gartley, three basic virtues are suggested for trading.

1. Patience to wait for the market formation to develop

2. Courage to put the order in and a protective stop to minimize risk.

3. Fortitude and temperament to sell
short. Again protecting the positions
with stops.

The "222" is one of the best patterns a
trader can expect. When it does not work it
usually means that a greater trend continuation is in progress. Failure of the "222" pattern
can be anticipated in several ways:

1. The presence of a huge gap near the D
termination point.

2. Wide range price ranges as point D is
forming.

3. After the formation of point D the
market fails to reverse. This may indi-
cate a level of consolidation before re-
suming the trend.

March S&P 500
5 minute

Gartley "222" Pattern

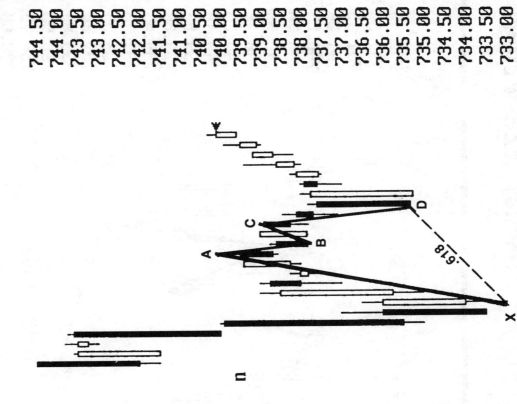

744.50
744.00
743.50
743.00
742.50
742.00
741.50
741.00
740.50
740.00
739.50
739.00
738.50
738.00
737.50
737.00
736.50
736.00
735.50
735.00
734.50
734.00
733.50
733.00

Interpretation of the Gartley "222" Pattern

This is not a "222" pattern in the classical Gartley interpretatiaon. The reason lies in the BC swing for two reasons: 1) Not enough time is contained in the BC swing. It should be at least five time bars. 2) The BC swing should be a .618 of AB. Finally, the CD move has extended way beyond the 1.618 of BC.

March S&P 500
1 minute

Gartley "222" Pattern

This is a one minute S&P chart illustrating the "222" pattern. It can be used as an entry technique. I do not recommend trading a one minute chart! What is important is to recognize the "222" on any time frame. On this particular day (January 4, 1997), the S&P 500 went 16 points down then reversed, closing up (a 36 point intraday swing).

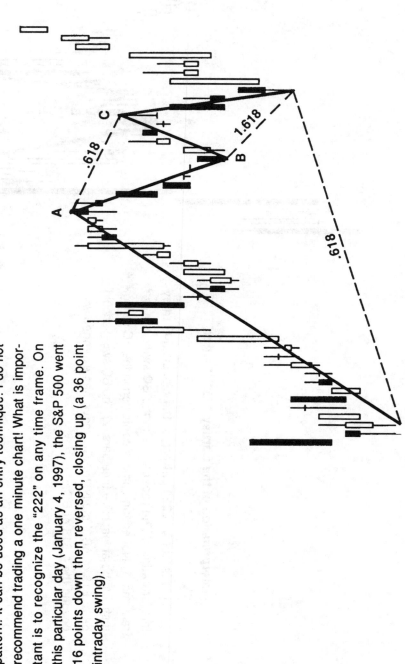

| 741.45 |
| 741.30 |
| 741.15 |
| 741.00 |
| 740.85 |
| 740.70 |
| 740.55 |
| 740.40 |
| 740.25 |
| 740.10 |
| 739.95 |
| 739.80 |
| 739.65 |
| 739.50 |
| 739.35 |
| 739.20 |
| 739.05 |
| 738.90 |
| 738.75 |
| 738.60 |
| 738.45 |
| 738.30 |
| 738.15 |
| 738.00 |

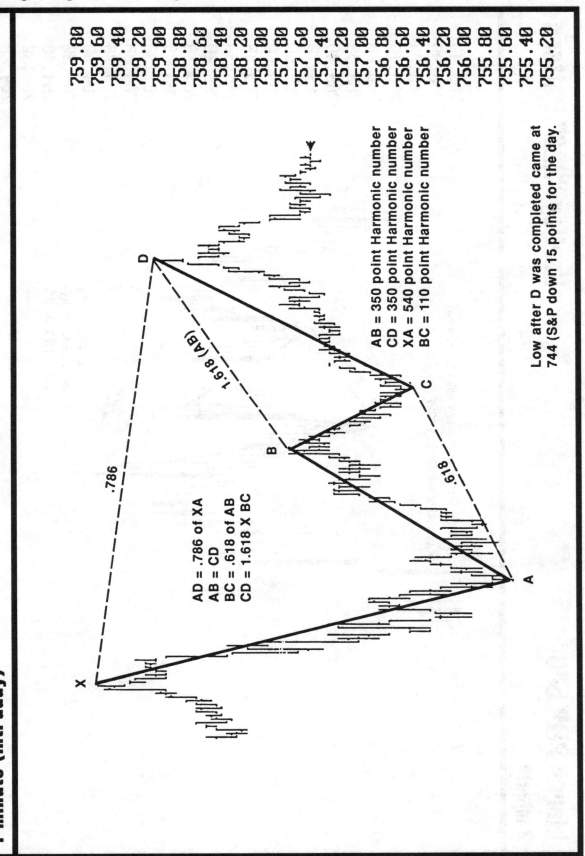

March S&P 500
1 minute (Intraday)

Gartley "222" Pattern

759.80
759.60
759.40
759.20
759.00
758.80
758.60
758.40
758.20
758.00
757.80
757.60
757.40
757.20
757.00
756.80
756.60
756.40
756.20
756.00
755.80
755.60
755.40
755.20

1.618 (AB)

.786

.618

AD = .786 of XA
AB = CD
BC = .618 of AB
CD = 1.618 X BC

AB = 350 point Harmonic number
CD = 350 point Harmonic number
XA = 540 point Harmonic number
BC = 110 point Harmonic number

Low after D was completed came at
744 (S&P down 15 points for the day.

March S&P 500
2 minute

Gartley "222" Pattern

This illustrates the low risk/high reward potential of the Gartley "222."

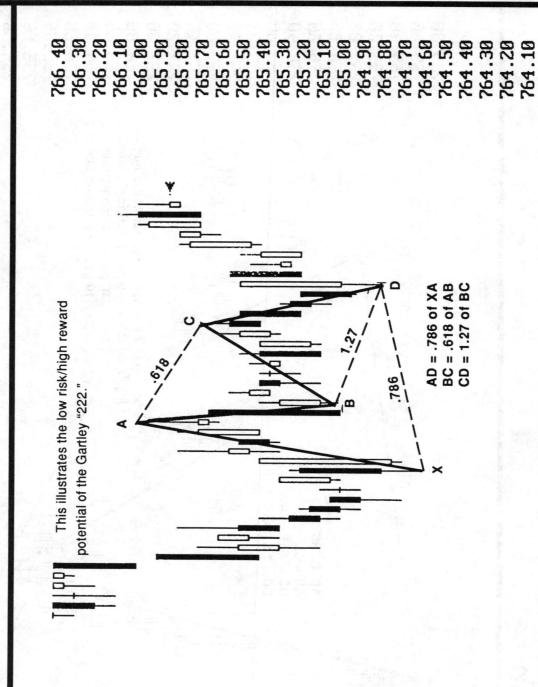

AD = .786 of XA
BC = .618 of AB
CD = 1.27 of BC

766.40
766.30
766.20
766.10
766.00
765.90
765.80
765.70
765.60
765.50
765.40
765.30
765.20
765.10
765.00
764.90
764.80
764.70
764.60
764.50
764.40
764.30
764.20
764.10

March S&P 500
2 minute

Gartley "222" Pattern

767.60
767.40
767.20
767.00
766.80
766.60
766.40
766.20
766.00
765.80
765.60
765.40
765.20
765.00
764.80
764.60
764.40
764.20
764.00
763.80
763.60
763.40
763.20
763.00

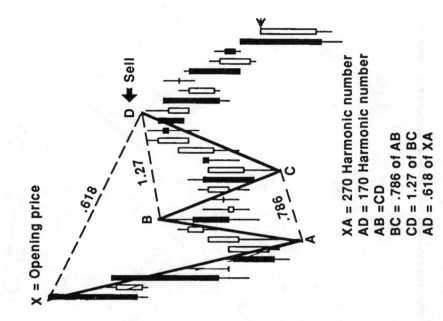

X = Opening price

Sell

D

.618

1.27

B

C

.786

A

XA = 270 Harmonic number
AD = 170 Harmonic number
AB = CD
BC = .786 of AB
CD = 1.27 of BC
AD = .618 of XA

This "222" was further enchanced by the fact that the sell signal at D was below the opening price.

You should be trading below the opening price which should be the high of the day more than 80 percent of the time. (See Opening Price chapter.)

March S&P 500
5 minute

Gartley "222" Pattern

This "222" was found by retracing .786 of the early daily range above the opening price. Remember: Buy above or sell below the opening price.

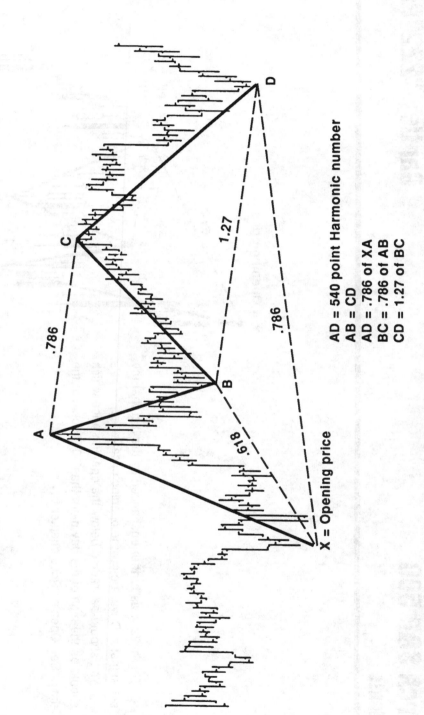

| 769.00 |
| 768.50 |
| 768.00 |
| 767.50 |
| 767.00 |
| 766.50 |
| 766.00 |
| 765.50 |
| 765.00 |
| 764.50 |
| 764.00 |
| 763.50 |
| 763.00 |
| 762.50 |
| 762.00 |
| 761.50 |
| 761.00 |
| 760.50 |
| 760.00 |
| 759.50 |
| 759.00 |
| 758.50 |
| 758.00 |
| 757.50 |

.786

1.27

.786

.618

X = Opening price

AD = 540 point Harmonic number
AB = CD
AD = .786 of XA
BC = .786 of AB
CD = 1.27 of BC

March S&P 500
5 minute

Gartley "222" Pattern

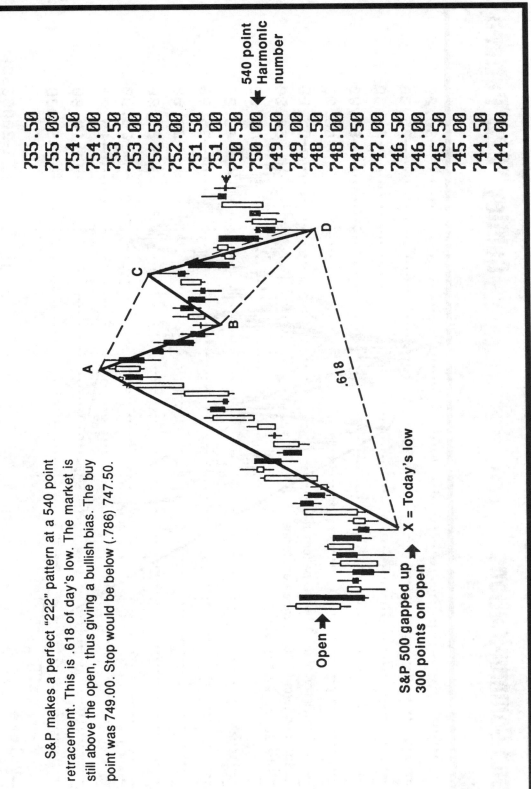

755.50
755.00
754.50
754.00
753.50
753.00
752.50
752.00
751.50
751.00
750.50
750.00 ← 540 point Harmonic number
749.50
749.00
748.50
748.00
747.50
747.00
746.50
746.00
745.50
745.00
744.50
744.00

S&P makes a perfect "222" pattern at a 540 point retracement. This is .618 of day's low. The market is still above the open, thus giving a bullish bias. The buy point was 749.00. Stop would be below (.786) 747.50.

.618

X = Today's low

S&P 500 gapped up 300 points on open

Open

Ascend Communications
Weekly

Gartley "222" Pattern

Completion of the AB = CD pattern at
the long term (.786) retracement forms
the Gartley "222" pattern.

A

C

B

1.618

D

1.27

.786

80.00
75.00
70.00
65.00
60.00
55.00
50.00
45.00
40.00
35.00
30.00
25.00
20.00
15.00
10.00
5.000

20000000
15000000
10000000
5000000
0

Volume

1995   1996   1997   1998

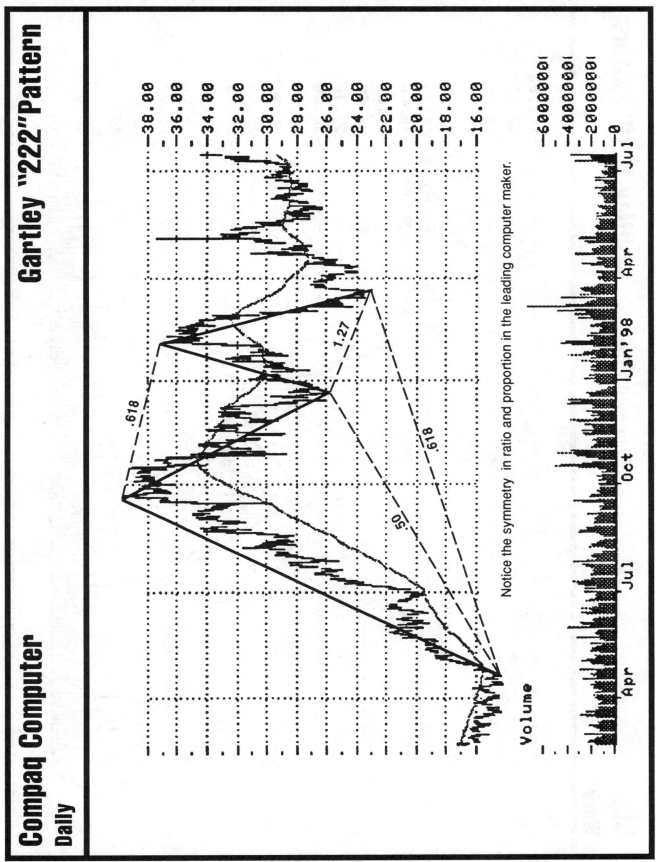

Compaq Computer
Daily

Gartley "222" Pattern

.618

1.27

.618

.50

Notice the symmetry in ratio and proportion in the leading computer maker.

Volume

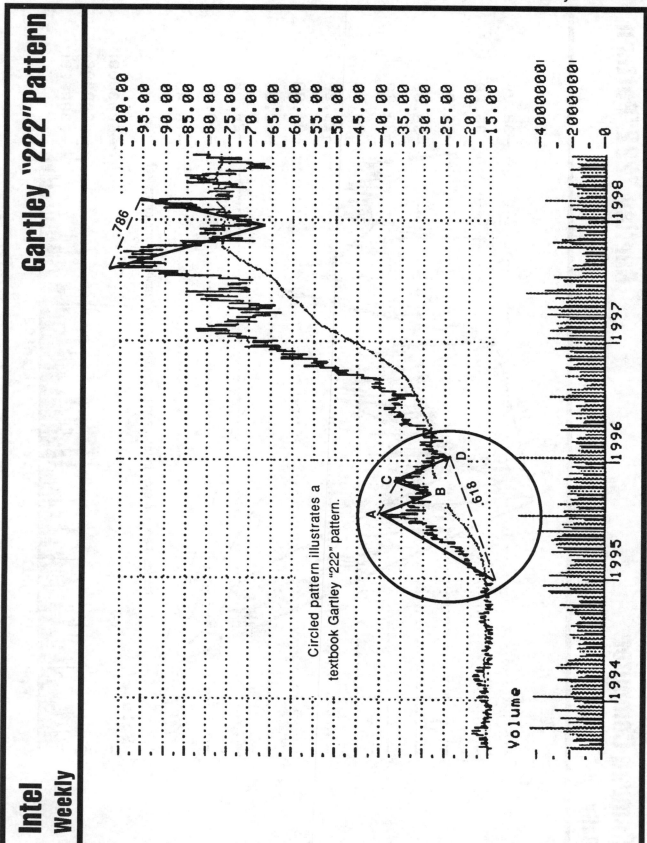

Gartley "222" Pattern

Intel
Weekly

Circled pattern illustrates a
textbook Gartley "222" pattern.

Dow Jones Industrials
5 minute

This is NOT a Gartley "222" Pattern

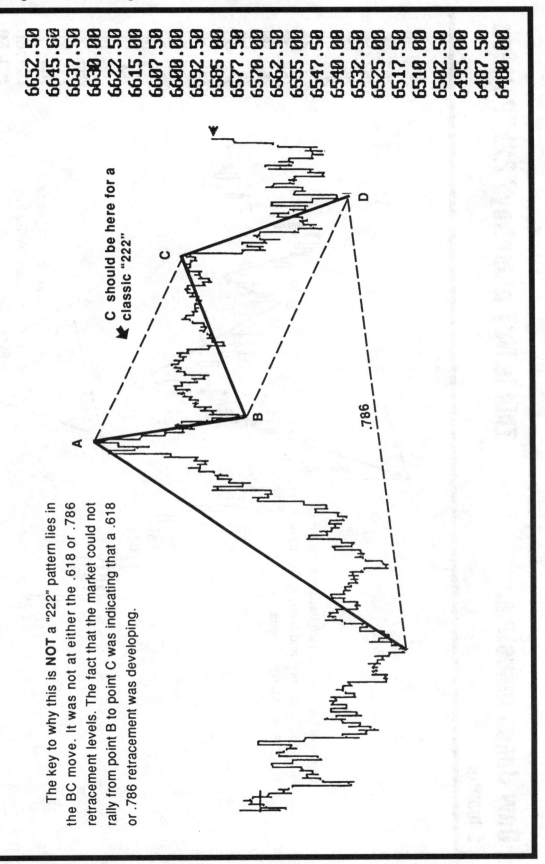

The key to why this is **NOT** a "222" pattern lies in the BC move. It was not at either the .618 or .786 retracement levels. The fact that the market could not rally from point B to point C was indicating that a .618 or .786 retracement was developing.

C should be here for a classic "222"

.786

6652.50
6645.60
6637.50
6630.00
6622.50
6615.00
6607.50
6600.00
6592.50
6585.00
6577.50
6570.00
6562.50
6555.00
6547.50
6540.00
6532.50
6525.00
6517.50
6510.00
6502.50
6495.00
6487.50
6480.00

Dow Jones Industrials
5 minute

This is NOT a Gartley "222" Pattern

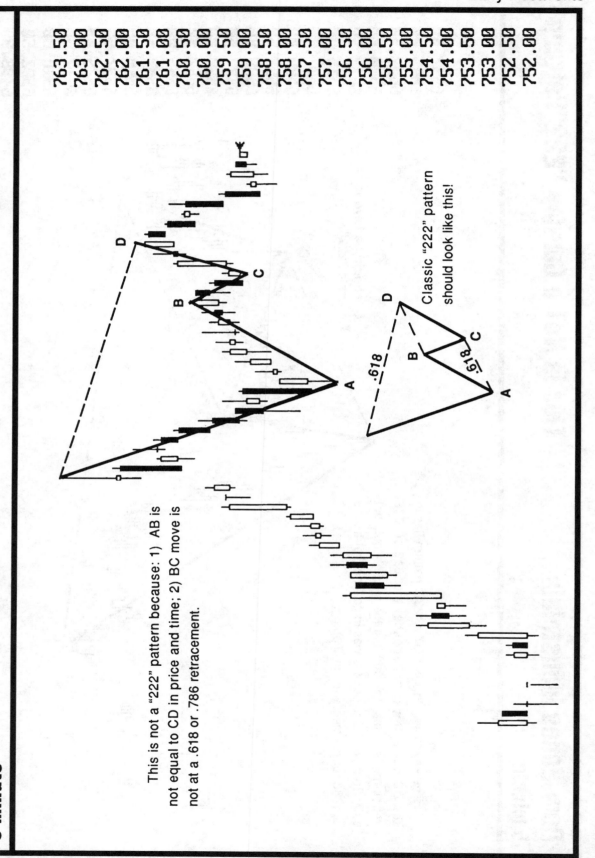

763.50
763.00
762.50
762.00
761.50
761.00
760.50
760.00
759.50
759.00
758.50
758.00
757.50
757.00
756.50
756.00
755.50
755.00
754.50
754.00
753.50
753.00
752.50
752.00

This is not a "222" pattern because: 1) AB is not equal to CD in price and time; 2) BC move is not at a .618 or .786 retracement.

Classic "222" pattern should look like this!

.618

.618

Dow Jones Industrials
5 minute

Failure of a Gartley "222" Pattern

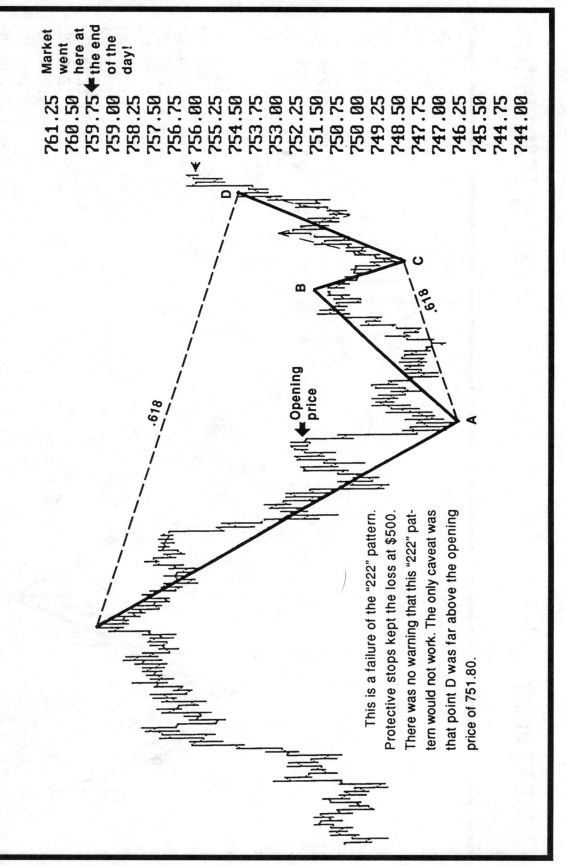

Market went here at the end of the day!

761.25
760.50
759.75 ←
759.00
758.25
757.50
756.75
756.00
755.25
754.50
753.75
753.00
752.25
751.50
750.75
750.00
749.25
748.50
747.75
747.00
746.25
745.50
744.75
744.00

.618

.618

Opening price

This is a failure of the "222" pattern. Protective stops kept the loss at $500. There was no warning that this "222" pattern would not work. The only caveat was that point D was far above the opening price of 751.80.

NASDAQ Index
Daily

Gartley "222"Pattern

March S&P 500
5 minute

Formation of the Gartley "222" Pattern

This is a potential "222" pattern in the making. There are three reasons why a short sale should be avoided today: 1) Prices are far above the opening price (12 points); 2) No time symmetry in AB = CD; 3) There are only two hours left in the trading day.

← Opening price (limit down) - 12 points

770.00
769.00
768.00
767.00
766.00
765.00
764.00
763.00
762.00
761.00
760.00
759.00
758.00
757.00
756.00
755.00
754.00
753.00
752.00
751.00
750.00
749.00
748.00
747.00

March S&P 500
5 minute

Failure of the Gartley "222" Pattern

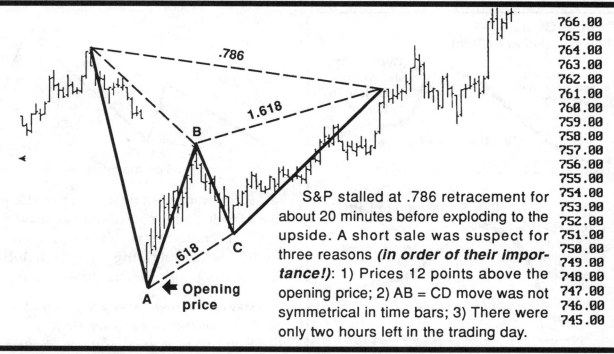

← Opening price

S&P stalled at .786 retracement for about 20 minutes before exploding to the upside. A short sale was suspect for three reasons *(in order of their importance!)*: 1) Prices 12 points above the opening price; 2) AB = CD move was not symmetrical in time bars; 3) There were only two hours left in the trading day.

766.00
765.00
764.00
763.00
762.00
761.00
760.00
759.00
758.00
757.00
756.00
755.00
754.00
753.00
752.00
751.00
750.00
749.00
748.00
747.00
746.00
745.00

Appendix II

Some Practical Tips on Cycles

Cycles are a funny lot—
Totally random they are not—
Just when you think you have a great find—
Along comes another to challenge your mind.

                                                                    –S.W.S.

The above poem sums up the study of cycles. I believe that speculation markets are non-random and chaotic. Within this chaos are respectable patterns of price and time. My Tomahawk neural network program has shown this to be true on a very consistent basis.

There are two cycle principles that I think each trader should explore. These were first brought to my attention when I studied Jim Hurst's Cyclitic material in 1971. The first principle is that of high translation. This means that bearish and bullish cycles have distinct characteristics.

The second cycle principle is that of nominality. Cycles usually repeat in equal increments. For instance, if there is a 9 period cycle it will usually repeat for at least 2 cycles = 18 periods. On occasion it will repeat for more than 5 cycles (5 waves) but then it will shift. The trader can learn two valuable lessons from this phenomenon. First, once the cycle has changed begin to look for the new nominal cycle. Second, once a nominal cycle has been identified keep using it until it stops working. That certainly sounds simple enough.

The study of cycles can be improved by using the principles of rational proportion. If you think of a price chart on any stock and commodity as nothing more than a road map, then all you have to do is to connect the dots to get to the destination. The following diagram is an oversimplification of what I'm trying to convey.

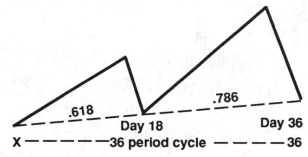

If the trader (analyst) will use the principle of ratio and proportion it can leave valuable clues as to the validity of a cycle. Reminder—we are dealing with probabilities only. Nothing is written as absolute law.

Take care of your losses and your profits
will take care of themselves.

                              —Amos Hostetter, Commodity Corp.

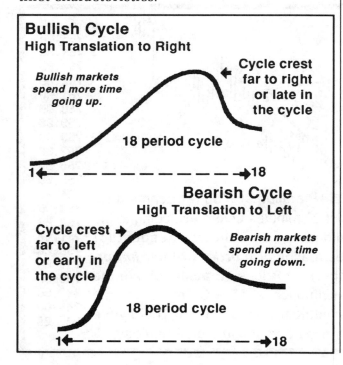

Fibonnaci Trading Card

My method of trading while on the floor of the CME was actually quite simple. Each night I would prepare the next day's trading from my apartment at McClurg Court. I kept daily charts on about 20 commodities and intraday charts on all major CME futures contracts. While on the floor, I would still trade Silver and Soybeans regularly, but the bulk of trading was in T-Bills and Gold. Later, it would be in the S&P 500 pit, but that wasn't traded until April of 1982. Because I did not like to enter the pits to trade for myself, I would physically hand the pit broker my order. I kept a swing chart on a trading card in my jacket. This is what it would look like:

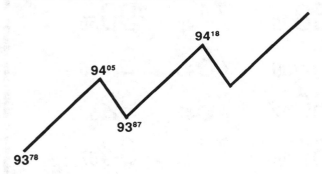

As prices would approach my buying or selling points I would watch the "runners" bringing orders into the pit from their respective commission houses. During a sharp rally or sell-off, this activity is really easy to see. As the activity slackened I would then move to the pit and take the opposite side (sell rallies — buy dips). I used a trading card with all of the Fibonacci numbers and the .618 and 1.618 relationships. As I mentioned earlier, I did not know the importance of the square roots of these numbers until 1989. The following 2 pages are a replica of the trading card I carried. I've included a card with the .786 and 1.27 relationships for your convenience. I still use these cards to this day, but now they are much larger and are placed on wooden frames hanging over my desk.

Notice the price of the S&P in the chart. That is the price it was trading at in 1982-83. The nearby futures would routinely trade at a discount to the cash S&P.

FIBONACCI TRADING CARD .618/1.618

06_{04}	21_{13}	37_{23}	52_{32}	68_{42}	84_{52}
07_{04}	22_{14}	38_{23}	53_{33}	69_{43}	85_{53}
08_{05}	23_{14}	39_{24}	54_{33}	70_{43}	86_{53}
09_{06}	24_{15}	40_{25}	55_{34}	71_{44}	87_{54}
10_{06}	25_{15}	41_{25}	56_{35}	72_{44}	88_{54}
11_{07}	26_{16}	42_{26}	57_{35}	73_{45}	89_{55}
12_{07}	27_{17}	43_{27}	58_{36}	74_{46}	90_{56}
13_{08}	28_{17}	44_{27}	59_{36}	75_{46}	91_{56}
14_{09}	29_{18}	45_{28}	60_{37}	76_{47}	92_{57}
15_{09}	30_{19}	46_{28}	61_{38}	77_{48}	93_{57}
16_{10}	31_{19}	47_{29}	62_{38}	78_{48}	94_{58}
17_{11}	32_{20}	48_{30}	63_{39}	79_{49}	95_{59}
18_{11}	33_{20}	49_{30}	64_{40}	80_{49}	96_{59}
19_{12}	34_{21}	50_{31}	65_{40}	81_{50}	97_{60}
20_{12}	35_{21}	51_{32}	66_{41}	82_{51}	98_{61}
	36_{22}		67_{41}	83_{51}	99_{61}

Example: 35_{21}   *Multiply $35 \times .618 = 21$*   *Add $21 + 35 = 56$ (1.618 of 35)*

FIBONACCI TRADING CARD   .786/1.27

4 05 6	17 21 27	29 37 47	42 53 67	54 69 88	67 85 108
5 06 8	17 22 28	30 38 48	42 54 69	55 70 89	68 86 109
6 07 9	18 23 29	31 39 50	43 55 70	56 71 90	68 87 110
6 08 10	19 24 30	31 40 51	44 56 71	57 72 91	69 88 112
7 09 11	20 25 32	32 41 52	45 57 72	57 73 93	70 89 113
8 10 13	20 26 33	33 42 53	46 58 74	58 74 94	71 90 114
9 11 14	21 27 34	34 43 55	46 59 75	59 75 95	72 91 116
9 12 15	22 28 36	35 44 56	47 60 76	60 76 97	72 92 117
10 13 17	23 29 37	35 45 57	48 61 77	61 77 98	73 93 118
11 14 18	24 30 38	36 46 58	49 62 79	61 78 99	74 94 119
12 15 19	24 31 39	37 47 60	50 63 80	62 79 100	75 95 121
13 16 20	25 32 41	38 48 61	50 64 81	63 80 102	75 96 122
13 17 22	26 33 42	39 49 62	51 65 83	64 81 103	76 97 123
14 18 23	27 34 43	39 50 64	52 66 84	64 82 104	77 98 124
15 19 24	28 35 44	40 51 65	53 67 85	65 83 105	78 99 126
16 20 25	28 36 46	41 52 66	53 68 86	66 84 107	

Example: 28 36 46   *Multiply*   36 x .786 = 28   36 x 1.27 = 46

S&P 500   Interrelationship of Waves

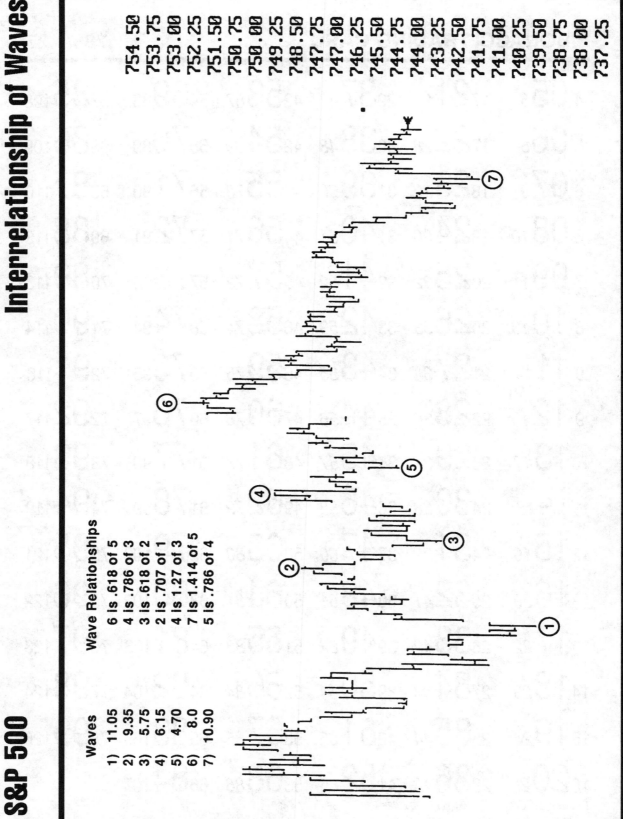

Waves

	Waves	Wave Relationships
1)	11.05	6 is .618 of 5
2)	9.35	4 is .786 of 3
3)	5.75	3 is .618 of 2
4)	6.15	2 is .707 of 1
5)	4.70	4 is 1.27 of 3
6)	8.0	7 is 1.414 of 5
7)	10.90	5 is .786 of 4

754.50
753.75
753.00
752.25
751.50
750.75
750.00
749.25
748.50
747.75
747.00
746.25
745.50
744.75
744.00
743.25
742.50
741.75
741.00
740.25
739.50
738.75
738.00
737.25

Appendix III

Some More Practical Tips

Money Management

I. Money management in risk speculation should be kept simple. Here are some unbreakable rules and some guidelines.
   A. Unbreakable Rules
      1. Never add to a losing position.
      2. Never risk **more than 10 percent** of your trading capital on any one trade.
      3. Always have a protective stop in place.
      4. If you don't have a profit in three days, exit the trade.
   B. Guidelines
      1. Never close a trade without a reason.
      2. Take 100 percent responsibility for your trades.
      3. Markets that have higher lows are in uptrends. Markets that have lower highs are in downtrends.
      4. Always do your analysis prior to the market open.

II. Ask these questions before closing a position:
   A. Does the position show a loss?
   B. Has it reached the price objective?
   C. Are you convinced your opinion is wrong?
      If the answer to all three questions is **NO**, then you **must hold** your position. If the answer to any one of the three is a **YES**, then you **may** close the trade if you wish.

III. Observations
   A. Calculate your trading capital and multiply by three percent. This will give you the amount of loss you can take on any trade. Example: $10,000 x 3% = $300. You should only risk $300 on the trade.
   B. As your account grows you must still use the three percent guideline, but you can trade more contracts.
   C. If you are able to trade multiple contracts you should consider using a "trailing" stop on one of the positions. This brings the risk closer to break-even.
   D. The trader must always protect himself from his own fallibility. Stops are placed for protection against yourself.

Markets are seldom wrong: men often are.

—Roy Longstreet

IV. Recommended reading
   A. Reminiscences of a Stock Operation, Edwin Lefevre
   B. The Disciplined Trader, Mark Douglass
   C. The Warrior Athlete, Dan Millman
   D. The Art of War, Sun Tsu
   E. The Psychology of Winning, Dennis Waitley

Life is a do-it-yourself project.

Controlled Risk
Money Management

30,000 x 10% = 3,000	$Risk	%Risk
#1 Money Contract	1,000	3 1/3%
#2 Trading Contract	1,000	3 1/3%
#3 Long Term Contract	1,000	3 1/3%

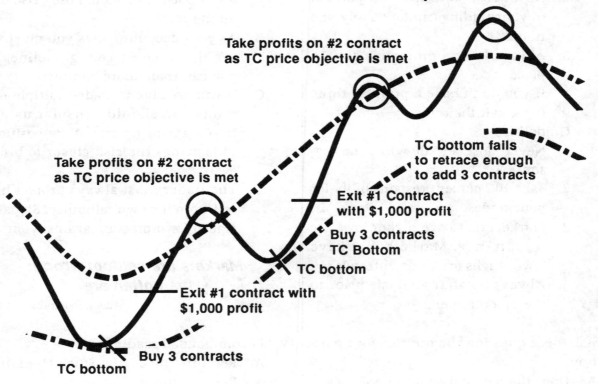

Take profits on both #3 contracts as long term price objectives are met

Take profits on #2 contract as TC price objective is met

Take profits on #2 contract as TC price objective is met

TC bottom fails to retrace enough to add 3 contracts

Exit #1 Contract with $1,000 profit

Buy 3 contracts TC Bottom

TC bottom

Exit #1 contract with $1,000 profit

Buy 3 contracts

TC bottom

This chart is courtesy of Walter Bressert. Mr. Bressert is a pioneer in cycle research and a director of the Foundation for the Study of Cycles. The chart is presented to alert our readers of the importance of risk control in trading all markets.

Danger Signals

Markets are seldom wrong! There is one fact that is always present in the markets: If prices go up there are more buyers; if prices go down there are more sellers. Here are a few technical indicators that suggest a market may be changing character:

Gaps:

A big price gap on a chart is indicative of a change in sentiment and deserves your attention. Use the Shapiro Iteration (wait one time-bar) before acting.

Wide Range:

When price ranges become abnormally wide, then price objectives are more likely to be exceeded (1.618). You should know the average daily range of the commodity you are trading.

Tail Close:

Markets that close at the extreme top or bottom are indicating strength or weakness. Look for several days of tail closes in the same direction.

Take care of your losses and the profits will take care of themselves.

—Amos Hostetter
Commodity Corporation (c. 1967)

Rules of Jesse Livermore
excerpted from *Reminiscences of a Stock Operator* by Edwin LeFevre

1. Of all the speculative blunders, there are few greater than trying to average a losing game.

2. Always sell what shows you a loss and keep what shows you a profit.

3. You cannot try to force the market into giving you something it does not have to give.

4. The courage in a specualtor is merely the confidence to act on the decision of his mind.

5. A loss never bothers me after I take it. I forget it overnight. But being wrong—not taking the loss—that is what does the damage to the pocketbook and to the soul.

6. The man who is right always has two forces working in his favor—basic conditions and the men who are wrong.

7. The trend is evident to a man who has an open mind and reasonably clear sight. It is never wise for a speculator to fit his facts to his theories.

8. In a narrow market when price moves within a narrow range, the thing to do is watch the market, read the tape to determine the limits of prices, and make up your mind that you will not take an interest until the price breaks through the limit in either direction.

9. You watch the market with one objective: to determine the direction or price ten-

dency. Prices like everything else, move along the line of least resistance.

10. In the long run commodtiy prices are governed but by one law—the economic law of supply and demand.

11. It costs me millions to learn that a dangerous enemy to a trader is his susceptibility to the urging of a magnetic personality combined with a brilliant mind.

12. Have a profit—forget it! Have a loss, forget it even quicker!

13. It never was my thinking that made the big money for me. It was always my sitting, my sitting tight.

14. There is only one side to the stock market and it is not the bull side or the bear side, but the right side.

HE WHO KNOWS NOT WHAT HE RISKS...RISKS ALL!

There are three rules you need to develop in order to trade successfully:

1. Build a foundation of trust in yourself so that you will act in your own best interests—without hesitation.

2. Follow a set of steps that will build confidence and a belief in your own consistency. This includes learning to not give your money away.

3. Execute your trades flawlessly when a signal is given. Ask yourself these three questions:

a. Is it an identifiable pattern?
b. Are the sacred ratios present?
c. Can I afford to take the risk?

If the answer to these three questions is 'yes!' then you should take the trade.

Keep in mind these important factors:

1. Money management always takes precedent over any trading methodology. You must never expose yourself to unlimited risk. Stops are placed for protection against yourself.

2. Never get into a trade where the risk is unknown.

3. The mistake is not **being** wrong; the mistake is in **staying** wrong!

4. Fear causes us to narrow our focus of attention and distorts our perception of the environment.

5. Self-discipline is the ability of maintaining your focus of attention when all the things in the environment are in conflict.

6. Never let the market save you—you must save yourself. Use stops!

7. We deal in probabilities! The market is always greater than anything we can ever anticipate. No methodology of trading can tell you what is going to happen next. Profits come from string of trades and not from one particular trade.

8. Take care of hour losses and the profits will take care of themselves! Release yourself from being wrong or the fear of losing money. Trading is not a game of right or wrong, it is the process of making money.

9. Be rigid in your rules and flexible with your observations.

Appendix IV
Additional Reading

Art of War. Sun Tsu.

Astro Cycles in Speculative Markets. Jensen, L. (Lambert-Gann Publishing).

Astro-Cycles: The Trader's Viewpoint. Pesavento, Larry. (AstroCycles, 1988).

Astro-Economic Interpretation. Jensen, L. (Lambert-Gann Publishing).

Business Cycles Versus Planetary Movements. Langham, J.M. (Maghnal).

Capital Ideas: The Improbable Origins of Modern Wall Street. Bernstein, Peter. (New York Free Press, 1992).

Chaos and Order in the Capital Markets. Peters, Edgar. (John Wiley & Sons, 1991).

Commodity Futures Trading with Point and Figure. Maxwell, Joseph.

Cycles—The Science of Prediction. Daiken, Dewey. (Foundation Study of Cycles).

Cyclical Market Forecasting: Stocks and Grains. Langham, J.M. (Maghnal).

Divine Proportion. Huntley. (Dover Press).

Economic Cycles: Their Law and Course. Moore, H. (Macmillan).

Elliott Wave Principle. Prechter Robert. (New Classics Library).

Extraordinary Popular Delusions and the Madness of Crowds. Mackay, Chuck.

Fibonacci Applications and Strategies for Traders. Fischer, Robert.

Forecasting Financial Markets: The Truth Behind Technical Analysis. Plummer, Tony. (Kogan Page Ltd., London, 1990).

Forecasting Prices. Butaney, T.G. (Pearl Printing).

Geometry of Markets. Gilmore, Bryce T. (Bryce Gilmore & Assoc., Pty Ltd., Melbourne, Australia, 1989).

Geometry of Markets II. Gilmore, Bryce T. (Bryce Gilmore & Assoc., Pty Ltd., Melbourne, Australia, 1993).

Investing for Profit with Torque Analysis of Stock Market Cycles. Garrett, W. (Ruff Pub. 508-448-6739)

Investor's Guide to the Net. Farrell, Paul (John Wiley & Son).

Market Wizards: Interviews with Top Traders. Schwager, Jack D. (Simon & Schuster, 1989).

Mastering Elliott Wave. Neely, Glenn.

Mathematics of Money Management. Vince, Ralph.

Planetary Effects on Stock Market Prices. Langham, J.M. (Maghnal).

Planetary Harmonics of Speculative Markets. Pesavento, Larry. (Astro-Cycles, 1990).

Profit Magic of Stock Transactions Timing. Hurst, J. (Prentice Hall).

Profits in the Stock Market. Gartley, H.M. (Lambert-Gann Publishing).

Rocky Mountain Financial Workbook. Foster, W. (Box 1093, Reseda, CA 91355).

Secret Teaching of All Ages. Hall, M.P. (Philosophical Society of Los Angeles).

Stock and Commodity Trader's Handbook of Trend Determinators. Bayer, George. (Out of Print.)

Stock Market Prediction. Bradley. (Llewellyn Publishing).

Technical Analysis of the Futures Markets. Murphy, John

Technical Analysis of Stock Trends. Edwards and Magee

The Dimensions of Paradise: The Proportions and Symbolic Numbers of Ancient Cosmology. Mitchell, John. (Harper & Row, 1988)

The Disciplined Trader: Developing Winning Attitudes. Douglass, Mark (New York Institute of Finance, 1990)

The Kabala of Numbers. Sepherial (Newcastle).

The Magic Word. Gann, W.D. (Lambert-Gann Publishing).

The Major Works of R.N. Elliott. (New Classics Library).

The Outer Game of Trading. Koppel, Robert and Abell, Howard. (Proteus Publishing, 1974).

The Secret of the Ages. Collier, Robert.

Time Factors in the Stock Market. Bayer, George. (Out of print.)

Tunnel Through the Air. Gann, W.D. (Lambert-Gann Publishing).

TRADERS PRESS, INC.®
PO BOX 6206
Greenville, SC 29606
Books and Gifts
for Investors and Traders

Publishers of:

A Complete Guide to Trading Profits (Paris)
A Professional Look at S&P Day Trading (Trivette)
Beginner's Guide to Computer Assisted Trading (Alexander)
Channels and Cycles: A Tribute to J.M. Hurst (Millard)
Chart Reading for Professional Traders (Jenkins)
Commodity Spreads: Analysis, Selection and Trading Techniques (Smith)
Comparison of Twelve Technical Trading Systems (Lukac, Brorsen, & Irwin)
Day Trading with Short Term Price Patterns (Crabel)
Fibonacci Ratios with Pattern Recognition (Pesavento)
Geometry of Stock Market Profits (Jenkins)
Harmonic Vibrations (Pesavento)
How to Trade in Stocks (Livermore)
Hurst Cycles Course (J.M. Hurst)
Jesse Livermore: Speculator King (Sarnoff)
Magic of Moving Averages (Lowry)
Planetary Harmonics of Speculative Markets (Pesavento)
Point & Figure Charting (Aby)
Point & Figure Charting: Commodity and Stock Trading Techniques (Zieg)
Profitable Grain Trading (Ainsworth)
Reminiscences of a Stock Operator (Lefevre)
Stock Market Trading Systems (Appel & Hitschler)
Stock Patterns for Stock Trading (Rudd)
Study Helps in Point & Figure Techniques (Wheelan)
Technically Speaking (Wilkinson)
Technical Trading Systems for Commodities and Stocks (Patel)
The Professional Commodity Trader (Kroll)
The Taylor Trading Technique (Taylor)
The Traders (Kleinfeld)
The Trading Rule That Can Make You Rich* (Dobson)
Traders Guide to Technical Analysis (Hardy)
Trading Secrets of the Inner Circle (Goodwin)
Trading S&P Futures and Options (Lloyd)
Understanding Bollinger Bands (Dobson)
Understanding Fibonacci Numbers (Dobson)
Viewpoints of a Commodity Trader (Longstreet)
Wall Street Ventures & Adventures Through Forty Years (Wyckoff)
Winning Market Systems (Appel)

Please contact **Traders Press** to receive our current 100 page catalog describing these and many other books and gifts of interest to investors and traders.

800-927-8222 ~ Fax 864-298-0221 ~ 864-298-0222 ~ tradersprs@aol.com
http://www.traderspress.com